THE PRICE OF SILENCE

THE PRICE OF SILENCE

A memoir

PHYL HERBERT

Phyl Herbert.

For my only child.

ISBN: 978-1-7395705-8-3

MENMA BOOKS

www.menmabooks.eu

Ballyhillow, Leap, Skibbereen, County Cork, P81 RK51, Ireland.

Printed and bound in Ireland by

Inspire, Skibbereen, Co. Cork.

www.inspire.ie

CONTENTS

'Distance doesn't separate people, silence does.'

— Anon

'It takes years to remember feelings you make yourself forget.

— Cathy Sweeney, *Breakdown*

TREE RINGS

1. LARKFIELD

'She's lost her tongue,' someone said.

My father was dealing cards. The big people were sitting around the table, but everyone was looking at me

'It's under the bushes,' my mother said, pointing outside the window.

So I toddled out into the garden to search, not really knowing what a tongue looked like. A long line of bushes separated our garden from our neighbour's. My three-year-old self must have been expecting to find some treasure, perhaps left by the fairies. I walked along the line of bushes, keeping my eyes fixed on the ground. All I could see was dry clay and the tangles of furry roots. Something was beginning to dawn on me. A sort of realisation. Then I heard tapping on the living room window. When I looked up, I saw the faces of my mother and father and their card-playing friends. They were all laughing at me.

It dawned on me then that my tongue had been in my head all along and that it was meant for speaking.

Our home was in a new estate with the lovely name of Larkfield on the border of the city and the foothills of the Dublin Mountains. It was built on land that had belonged to the family of Joseph Plunkett, one of the leaders of the 1916 Rising, and it was here that the lads who came over from England and Scotland to join the Rising lived and trained. The cosy houses were built in the 1930s by public utility societies, a kind of public-private partnership between Dublin Corporation and various groups including unions and civil servants.

But that was well before I was born. My father used to say that the people who lived on our road were like Liquorice All-Sorts. 'A mixed bag,' he'd say, but I used to think that he was talking about our family.

My mother once told me that all our years were numbered inside us, like the rings inside a tree trunk. That each hour, each day, each season had its own hidden tale. The tales of bad winters and good summers were all written there too. So which ring was I at when I first began to observe the world change around me? Sometime around the sixth or seventh one I began to notice things changing, within me and without. There were, of course, things in my little world that didn't change, like my family, my house and my place at the table.

No, my place at the table never changed. I was always sat between two brothers on one side and my older sister on the other. Grown-ups loved asking me the names of my brothers and sisters. Were they trying to catch me out? Checking if I really belonged?

'Peggy, Mary, Kevin, Noel, Murty, Eamonn, Thomas, Eileen, Peter and Michael.'

'And what's your name, then?' they would say. 'Where do you come in?'

'I'm Phyl, and I'm in the middle. Five over and five under.'

There wasn't enough room for us all to sit together at the great mahogany table. In fact, I don't ever remember us all being together in the same room until the day of my mother's funeral. When that day came there would be another person there. Somebody nobody ever met before.

Well, that's not strictly true, because my sister had met her once, and so had my mother. And, of course, so had I.

But all of that was down the road. A long way down the road.

Our road was teeming with children. Joan lived on one side of our house and Dolores lived around the corner. These were my two best friends. We were known locally as the 'three little ones.'

The Halpins lived on the other side of our house. They had no children at all. My brother whispered to me one day that this was because they were

Protestants. Mrs Halpin was very kind, though. She brought jelly and ice-cream to my mother once a week.

'Get that into you, missus,' she'd say. 'You don't look after yourself.'

Her husband never spoke to us, and he always looked as if he was in a bad mood. Every time she spoke his name, she'd let out a little chuckle; it was like when she said, 'My Jim,' that she felt something tickling her. It wasn't funny to me, and I knew by the way my mother looked at her that it wasn't funny to her either.

A lot of the houses on our road were owned by Protestants, and I found out later that was how we got ours—it was because my father worked for them in their big houses in Terenure. My mother used to say that our father was meant to be an artist but that there was no money in that sort of thing. He was a great painter and could paint fancy stuff on their walls, stuff like marble stencilling and murals. When my father was in a good mood, he used to teach us how to paint on glass. The colours he used for mountains and fields were very unusual, a golden brown mixed with green. I think that was because he was a Dublin man and didn't know much about the real country.

Not like my mother, who was reared on a farm, and knew the names of trees and plants.

The man in the big house got my father a job in the Guinness Brewery as a painter and decorator. The man said, 'Arthur will look after your wife and children now.' For thirty-five years my father cycled to James's Gate Brewery, leaving in the early morning before we were out of bed. He never missed a day from work during those years.

My childhood days were spent playing on the road in front of our house or in someone's back garden. Occasionally the big girls and boys would take us to the sea, to Sandymount or Seapoint. The older girls would hold my hand and bring me far out into the water so that it was over my head and then one of them would lift me onto their hip and when a big wave rolled towards us she would glide over it and I would feel then that I could swim in the deep sea.

It was like I was flying on the water like a bird perched on its mother's wing.

We would come home with our towels and togs saturated with salty seawater and gritty beach sand. My mother would shake the towels and hang them out, until the wind dried them and the sand had fallen into the grass. Once or twice we were brought up the mountains, and on the way home, one of the big boys would give me a jockey-back.

2. A GAME

One warm sunny day during the school holidays, when we three, Joan, Dolores and me, were lying on the grass in my front garden, Joan said, 'let's make a daisy-chain.'

The grass was snow-white with the sparkling daisies, and we soon had enough to make our princess crowns.

Joan looked at mine and said, 'Mine is nicer than yours.'

And then Dolores said, 'No, mine is the nicest.'

Now, all our daisy chains were exactly the same, so I didn't say anything. Later on, we went out onto the road and Joan asked everybody passing, 'Which of us is the nicest looking?'

I realised for the first time that I didn't know what I looked like, and I thought that both my pals must look nicer than me. Of course, there was a big mirror in our house, but it was high up over the mantlepiece and I had no interest in it. We hadn't yet made our First Holy Communion.

All of our days were about playing and dreaming, and then some things happened that weren't about playing. Things that marked my childhood, things that clung like ivy, numbered out inside of me.

That day, Dolores's big sister Jacinta called us into her shed at the back of their garden. She was talking with her big friends. 'What game will we play today?'

She always had a fierce cross face on her, and when she talked it was like she was giving out. 'It's time you three little ones learned how to play proper games.'

We were excited to be invited and not to be seen as babies anymore.

'Don't tell anybody about what goes on in here.' Jacinta looked at me and then said in a strange voice, 'Do ya hear me?'

I knew that I was going to see something new now. But I couldn't imagine what. Then, suddenly, I didn't want to play her game. I had a bad feeling.

'Get in there!' Her voice was harder now.

It was dark inside the shed except for the gap at the side where the light splashed across the floor from a little crack in the wooden walls. Joan held Dolores's hand and I just followed behind them. Jacinta pulled the door shut behind us with such a bang that I jumped. All I could see now were shadowy figures. Jacinta stood in front of the crack in the shed wall and looked like she had suddenly grown a few inches. She put her hands in her pocket and took out a box of matches. I could see the word Friendly written in front of the red box. I thought it was a funny name for matches. She struck the match and lit a short stub of a candle.

'Now' she said, 'We're ready.'

I could see a little more now. Two other girls I didn't know were playing nurses, and a younger boy was lying on a bench in the middle of the floor. He was the patient, and Jacinta was the doctor. The name of the game was Doctors and Nurses.

'Pull your trousers down. I'm going to examine you.'

Nobody else spoke because this was Jacinta's game and she was in charge. Her voice filled the shed and hurt my ears. I didn't know the boy's name, but I knew him to see because he was in the same class as my brother. Jacinta was ten years of age and was taller than her two friends who were standing at either side of the bench. She pretended that the rope around her neck was a stethoscope and she kept pulling at it as she stared at the boy.

'Pull your trousers down,' she ordered.

Her big hands dug into his stomach and the boy started to cry. I felt sick now. Did she do that to the other boys in my brother's class? Who could I tell about this? The boy started to cry louder and was struggling to get off the bench.

'Shut up, will ya?' Her friends began to laugh.

Why wouldn't they help the boy? I was afraid to move. I couldn't look at Jacinta but I could hear her.

'Cry baby! Pull up your trousers and go home to your mammy.'

The boy ran out as fast as he could, still holding onto his unfastened trousers. Tears were smeared all over his face. I wanted to run after him and say I was sorry, but I couldn't move.

'He was no fun.' Jacinta made a funny noise, like a cackle.

Her mouth pursed, then she pulled back her lips to show her clenched teeth. I thought of a horse showing its teeth when it wasn't happy. She made an odd, hissing noise and I just wanted to run towards the door of the shed out into the light and home.

'Who's next?'

She took the piece of rope from around her neck and started swinging it around. I thought she was going to whip me with it. I started to make a move towards the door, very slowly. I could feel something pulling me back. When I turned around she was holding the end of my frock and sneering, showing her big teeth.

'Your dress is dirty, Take it off.'

I knew my dress wasn't dirty at all because it was only my first day wearing it. Her eyes were widening and her mouth was opened wide when I slowly took my dress off. I could feel her looking at every part of my body.

'And take off your knickers too.' I thought I must be dreaming. Why wasn't someone helping me or at least stopping Jacinta? Nobody spoke. All eyes were looking at me. There was nothing for it but to do as she said.

Standing there, without any clothes on I didn't know whether to shout or to cry. Then a wave of something came over me and I thought: I'm not going to let this horrible girl see me cry.

'Give her a dare.' It was the first time I heard one of the nurses speak.

Jacinta paused for a moment. Then she leaned down over me. 'Now young wan, I dare you to run to the front of our house and shout out to the first person who passes by.'

Joan and Dolores looked at me as if they didn't know who I was. Nobody moved. There was silence for a long time. I made a move to where my clothes were, but Jacinta put her foot on them and pointed to the front of the house. 'Go out there and shout out and then I'll give you these back.'

'Shout what?' I squeaked at her. I couldn't let her know I was afraid of her.

My heart was beating in panic. I knew I had to do it quickly before I could get dressed again and run home.

'Shout out "Look at me" to the first person who passes.'

Like a wound-up toy, I ran out towards the street. At first, blinking in the sunlight, I saw no one. I was relieved. Maybe Jacinta would let me off. Then, out of the blue, footsteps approached. It was a man.

It was Mr Halpin, our next-door neighbour, who never talked.

'Look...' I called out to him.

I couldn't say another word because he did look at me. Straight at me. He stopped dead in the street and his creepy green eyes moved over me, slowly, slowly, over my naked body, right down to my bare feet.

There was a sort of snarl in his voice. 'I'll tell your mother what you've been up to, young lady!' He turned on his heel, slapping the rolled-up newspaper sharply against his hip. But my dare was done. I raced back in off the street.

In the shed, Jacinta threw my dress and knickers at me and told me to get out of her garden. Why was she so angry now? I didn't understand any of it at all. Hadn't I done what she had ordered?

At teatime, later that day, I kept stealing secret glances over at my mother at the top of the table. Was there anything in her eyes that might tell me she knew something? Some sign that Mr Halpin had spoken to her. I watched her lips part slowly as she sipped a cup of tea thoughtfully, oblivious to the clatter and chatter all around her. That way she had of stroking her right temple before saying something important. She glanced over at me and smiled softly. 'Eat up, Phyl.'

No, there was nothing strange in the smile. She was just the same as she had been earlier. So Mr Halpin hadn't told on me. Maybe he was being nice to me. I still wanted to say something to my mother, though. But only when the others weren't there. That was never.

3. NIGHT WHISPERS

The next day, we three little ones were sitting by the wall at the side of our house. We were playing a game of marbles.

'I don't want to play with those big girls again,' I said, and my two friends looked at me and said together, 'Neither do we.'

Our side wall was facing the Halpins' living room window, and every so often it seemed like the net curtains were moving but I took no notice after a while because Joan had got a packet of new coloured marbles and she was dividing them out between me and Dolores. I was hoping she would give me the red ones, but I said nothing. We were busy putting the new marbles in a row when Mr Halpin appeared at the railing, without a word. He looked straight at me and pointed his finger as if to say 'You've been a bold girl.' I was waiting for him to say something else, but he didn't. Instead, he just picked me up as if I were an ornament on the mantelpiece and lifted me over the railing and carried me into his house.

My two friends went on playing as if this was what happened every day.

I had never been inside this house before. Mr Halpin pulled over the dusty, heavy curtains before sitting down on the big armchair. It was dark and I could barely see him. A chill ran over me and I started to cry.

'It's OK,' he said. 'I'll give you a biscuit in a minute.'

He pulled me onto his lap, took my hand and put it inside his trousers. I froze. The smell from his bald head was making me sick now because he was bending down near my face. I started to cry, but he kept pushing my small hand around and it all felt a bit sticky down there. Then, out of the blue, the doorbell rang. I felt like it was an angel coming to rescue me, but it was just his wife. Mr Halpin ran into the kitchen. He put a Mikado biscuit in each of my hands, brought me out the side door and lifted me back over the railing. I heard him tramp back through the house and open the door to his wife. Her cheery, innocent voice echoed along the hall.

The two girls looked up from their marbles and blinked at me. 'Where did you get the biscuits from?'

I said nothing. Just passed the biscuits to them silently and watched in a sort of daze as they went on playing marbles.

In school, we were preparing for our first confession, and I began to secretly ask myself what sin I had committed with Mr Halpin. Was there a separate word for it even? It wasn't stealing and it wasn't bearing false witness or taking the Lord's name in vain, whatever that really meant. At least, I didn't think it was. Would it come under impure thoughts? I didn't really know what impure meant either. I would have to think about it later. And I couldn't ask anyone, of course.

Our cousin Helen was coming to stay one night, not long after that. We were all excited because nobody ever stayed overnight in our house. Helen was our favourite cousin She wasn't afraid of anyone or anything, my mother said. Not even the huge horses they used for ploughing down on the farm in Wexford. And she was very clever.

'That one could teach a horse to talk, she's so cute,' my mother said.

Helen was on her way home to Wexford after her summer job in England. My mother said that England was a place across the water and it was a heathen country. England must be a place with watery roads where heather grew because that was what 'heathen' meant to me. Helen was very brave too. She wasn't afraid of getting on the boat by herself and working in the big hotel as a chambermaid during her school holidays.

I slept in the front room with my two older sisters. There were two big beds in the room. That night I slept at the bottom end of the bed, making space for my cousin at the top. Helen's suitcase was on the floor and so was the box that my communion dress was in. There was no stain on the white dress, but I knew I had a stain on my soul, which might be washed away now after my first confession. I was the first to go to bed and pretended to be asleep when they all arrived into the room. It was exciting to have a visitor and especially one who had been to England. The light was hurting my eyes so I put my head under the covers. I pretended to be asleep, but I nearly gave the game away when I felt Helen's cold feet against my back.

The whispering started when the light was turned out. I didn't understand all the words they used. But I knew they had to be talking about secrets and they were using bold words as well. Very bold words. You knew by the way they said them, in a low, whispery sort of voice.

Helen started talking about all the girls who worked in the hotel, and about one in particular.

'She had to send money home to her parents every week, but she didn't make enough in the hotel.'

'What did she do, then?' my big sister Peg asked.

'She got the offer of making loads of money, for only two hours work, in another place.'

'Where was that?'

'In a brothel.'

There was silence for a moment. Then my other sister Mary, who was only a year younger than Peg, asked, 'What's a brothel, Helen?'

I was glad she asked that question because I was getting really interested in this story now. My cousin said it was a place where you gave kisses to people and that you allowed them to touch your private parts. 'What are private parts?' I wanted to ask that now but I stayed quiet under the pillow.

'And one day,' my cousin continued, 'didn't her own brother walk in! He was her next customer.'

A shocked silence fell over our beds. I was bursting to scream out for more information. Then the dark room seemed to swallow up all the voices, and it became much harder to hear the whispers. Still, it was a long time before I fell asleep because I was trying to work out in my head all that had been said.

The next morning at breakfast, my mother asked Helen if she would like to live in England. Helen made a funny face and said 'No, Aunty Babs. I'd much prefer to stay in Holy Ireland.' She winked at me, and I wondered if she knew that I knew her secret.

After my cousin Helen left our house, I added a few more sins to my list for my first confession—the sin of showing off my body without clothes on and the sin of listening to my cousin's bold story and pretending to be asleep. Maybe Helen was the person to tell me what sin I had committed with Mr Halpin. I could ask her also was his house a brothel. There was no other person I could ask, not my mother or my sisters.

But I knew it was all marked down inside me, somewhere on the tree rings, somewhere in the soil I was rooted in.

4: WEXFORD

Like all of my siblings, I have romantic memories of my childhood summers in Wexford. Dylan Thomas's poem 'Fern Hill' captures it perfectly.

Now as I was young and easy under the apple boughs
About the lilting house and happy as the grass was green...

The days were always sunny, the haystacks like a Vincent Van Gogh painting, always a golden yellow. Red geraniums and pink hydrangeas blazing away in front of whitewashed garden walls. Chickens clucking in the farmyards, cows being milked and horses trotting by with their manes floating like ribbons in the air, their legs stretching out through the wide-open acres of grass. It was the perfect playground for a child from the city.

My first holiday in Wexford was just before my eighth birthday. My mother put me onto the train at Westland Row Station with my little brown case packed. I would be met at Killurin station by my cousin. 'Be a good girl, Phyl, and don't let me down now.'

This was my mother's territory and these were my mother's people. She was born in the house on the hill, the youngest member of her family, hence her name Babs. Her three sisters lived down in the valley. Moll and Nan lived together on a small farm, both unmarried. Some of my siblings stayed with them during the summer. I always stayed with my Aunt Nell and Uncle Davey just up the road, because one of their daughters, Sena, was my own age. My Aunt Nell ran a shop in the front part of her house. When a customer arrived, a bell would ring that she could hear from her kitchen. All the young people of the area gathered there every evening.

This particular summer, I learned a few new facts about my mother's life. I had never met my grandmother, because she died when I was a baby, but I heard from Moll and Nan that when she was young she had emigrated to America during the Spanish Flu epidemic after the First World War. Her stay in that faraway place was cut short when she bumped into someone from Wexford who informed her that her mother had fallen ill.

My Aunt Nan looked at me when she told me that and said, 'If she had stayed in America, you wouldn't be here now.'

It took me a long time to figure that one out. I loved listening to Nan. She was always talking about the sort of life that people lived.

She would say, 'People are quare strange, the things they might do.'

Her eyes were the brownest I'd ever seen, and I always had the feeling that those eyes could see things that nobody else could. When she was talking to you, she looked right into your soul. You wouldn't dare tell her a lie.

It didn't matter how hot the day was, the fire would always be burning away under that big chimney breast. Most of the cooking was done over that fire, in a big round black pot called a skillet. Nan would turn the wheel in the corner with the leather strap around it to make the flames stronger, pulling on her Woodbine cigarette. She could talk and smoke at the same time as she turned the bellows wheel. That first summer, she came out with another fact.

'Your mother was the best-looking girl in these parts. She could have married anyone! And then she had to go and marry a Dublin Jackeen.' She paused for a moment and gave me one of the smiles that made her eyes twinkle.

'Mind you, you wouldn't be here either, Phyl, if she had married one of her admirers.'

Many years later, after my father's death, when I began to visit my mother every Sunday, she told me that as a young girl she loved to help out at threshing time, when the local men came to the farm to help with the work.

It was my mother's job to bring the basket of food to the fields at lunchtime. She told me of the day when one of the men—who wasn't a local, as it happened—stood stock still and looked at her for a long time, then said, 'Young girl, when you are a little older I'm going to come back and marry you.' In her innocence she looked out for the man at the next few threshings. But he never returned.

I loved learning new country words like 'threshing' and 'haggard.' The haggard was the area of land opposite Moll and Nan's house, where early vegetables were grown. It was a sort of kitchen garden. There were apple and plum trees at the end of it, and the chickens roamed free around the grass. Moll and Nan had their cow-house beside the haggard. Moll did all the milking and made butter in her dairy, a small building beside the house. Sometimes she let me turn the handle of the churn and, when the butter was ready, she would let me pat it into balls with the wooden spatulas. Wexford butter was much nicer than Dublin butter, particularly on mashed potatoes. Aunt Nell sold some of the butter in her shop because she had a fridge for ice-cream.

Nan would often come to the shop on her bicycle for her Woodbine cigarettes and snuff for her sister. My cousin Sena told me that Moll never left the house, except for first mass on Sundays, and that was because she had a baby who didn't have any father. That was another thing that I had to work out that summer. It was a big scandal at the time, but Moll loved her daughter. And when that daughter left for England to work, at the age of fourteen, poor Moll was broken-hearted.

I would never let things like that happen to me.

Sena was the youngest in her family, and her mother never said a cross word to her, or to anyone else, for that matter. Aunt Nell was always in a good mood. She was a tiny woman with a big heart, and her husband, Uncle Davey, was a big man who adored his wife. Uncle Davey was a builder and he left the house early every morning for work. Myself and Sena would be in bed when he got home but we would hear him saying the Rosary with Aunt Nell at the same time every night, below in the kitchen.

'Hail Mary, Holy Mary,' was all we could hear, because he spoke very fast. The hissing and murmuring of voices reminded me of the bee sounds that I heard passing the hives at the back of the house. That area was out of bounds for us, and the only person allowed to go there was Uncle Davey. He could talk to the bees, and they never stung him because he had a very gentle voice.

After breakfast each morning, we would race to see who would collect the most eggs from the henhouse. At first I was afraid to go inside because some of the hens would be standing high up on the roost bar. They would sometimes flap their wings at me, so I would look for eggs under the hedges outside the house instead.

'You're afraid of your shadow,' Sena would say. Or 'Dublin Jackeen. What do they teach you up there?' But as the days passed and I became braver I would answer her back. 'I'll show you I'm not afraid, you Wexford Yellow Belly.' Then we would both laugh.

In the afternoon, we often visited Murphy's, the next farm to the shop. Before going into the big redbrick house we would drop in to the milking parlour where Lawrence Murphy and the farmhands milked the cows. Lawrence had a smile that always made you feel welcome. When he smiled, his eyes shone a brighter shade of blue. Sena used to tease him about all the girls he chatted to at the night-time gatherings outside the shop.

His reply was always the same, 'I can't help it, girl, if I'm good-looking.' He would turn the teat of the cow and squirt milk at her then. I would just stand there looking at the big udders on the cows. 'Go away up to the house with ye, now!'

Mrs Murphy's smiling face always lifted my spirits. The first time I met her, she said, 'Now, I'm going to let our visitor from Dublin choose her own cup and saucer.'

She took me by the hand and brought me up to the big parlour. Then she opened up the china cabinet. I had never seen so many coloured china cups before, each one more beautiful than the one behind it, each one waiting to be picked as my favourite. From that day onwards, the yellow cup and saucer with the blue cornflowers around the rim was called 'Phyl's cup.' Mrs Murphy's brown, smiling face looking at me felt like a big hug, and I always got the feeling that she liked me.

'Who did ye have up at the shop last night?'

She spoke to us like we were big girls. After a few weeks into my holidays, I got to know all the names of the people who would visit the shop, so I was able to answer her questions.

'Aren't ye getting more like us every day?' She let out a little laugh then and said, 'Will yourself and Sena keep an eye on my boy Lawrence when he's play-acting with those girls outside the shop? That lad is losing the run of himself.'

There was a little house outside the shop where the oil was kept, and hanging on the door was a ring board. Each number on the board had a hook. You threw a ring onto the hoop with the biggest number, and whoever got the highest score won the game. Only boys were allowed play. We used to sit on the garden wall and watch them.

One day I got up the courage and asked Mrs Murphy why girls didn't play rings. She looked at me for a long time and then let out a little giggle, 'Sure, ye would only be a distraction to those poor lads.'

One day when Sena and I were lying in the meadow looking up at the blue sky and wondering what lay beyond, we started to talk about what we would do when we grew up. We lay there for what seemed like hours. I remember feeling the wide-open expanse of the sky over my small frame and breathing in the colours of the poppies and the buttercups and the daisies and thinking what a beautiful world it was and that I wanted the moment to last forever.

The day of my return to Dublin was the day my world crumbled a little. Uncle Davey would come into the bedroom before going to work. 'Goodbye, allanah. Safe journey.' Then he would put a half-crown piece into my sleepy hand.

‘Thank you,’ I would say in a daze, thinking I was still dreaming and that I could stay here with Sena forever.

Later, Aunt Nell would leave me to the station and hold my hand in silence while we waited on the platform. We were both sad to be parting at the end of the holiday. ‘Sure, we’ll see you next year, please God.’

That particular summer my mother met me at Westland Row station. I could see her in the distance. I was hoping that she would notice my new dress that Aunt Nell made for me. I knew that she would love the pound of Wexford butter that I had in my case. I started to run towards her, hoping that she would wrap her arms around me and tell me how much she missed me. But when I got to her, she just put out her hand to shake mine, as if I was now a grown-up, and said ‘Welcome home.’

That was one of the two things I remember about my return to Dublin that summer. The second was my father’s greeting when I got into our house.

‘What are you doing, talking in this house with a Wexford accent, girl?’ And I hated the Dublin accent for evermore after that.

Decades later, I drove past the area where my cousin and I had lain in the meadow looking up at the sky all those years before. The meadow had been concreted over, and instead of poppies and buttercups, the field was covered with summer houses for rent. I thought about those two young girls who had asked the universe that summer who they were and what the future held in store for them.

5. THE NUNS

Sister Evangelist, Mother Superior of the Presentation Convent in Terenure, came into our class on the last day of the summer term. 'The Pres' stood just beyond Terenure crossroads, backing onto Eaton Square. It was a quiet, off-the-beaten-track sort of school, and Sister Evangelist ruled the roost. She was a very small figure of a nun, but she put the fear of God in everyone who knew her. Nobody ever saw her smile, and for a small person she left a huge wake of fear and anger in her trail. A wimple covered most of her face. All that could be seen were her darting brown eyes, pinched mouth and pointed chin.

We all knew the purpose of her visit this day: to announce the names of the six girls chosen to enter the secondary school. We stood up when she entered the classroom. Sister Evangelist nodded towards the teacher and beckoned to us to sit down. She steepled her fingers, then pointed them at the class, as if she were scouting for a target with her piercing eyes.

'As you know girls, there are only eighteen places in our first-year class in secondary school. We can only select six of the best girls from our three sixth year classes.'

She then proceeded to read out the names, not of girls who were the best in the class, but of those who came from the better-off families.

'That's not fair, sister! Those aren't the best girls.'

The words just tumbled out. I could not contain myself. Sister Evangelist had made a mistake, and it was this injustice that made me forget my shyness.

The teacher's eyes flashed with anger. 'Please sit down, Miss Herbert! You don't speak to the Reverend Mother like that!'

She then glanced over at Sister Evangelist. But I wasn't finished speaking yet. I was one of the non-chosen few and I knew, deep down, that I was beyond punishment. There were other plans for me.

I looked over at Antoinette Mahon, a girl who lived near me. Hadn't our teacher always said she was the best girl in the class?

'Why wasn't Antoinette chosen?' Antoinette went scarlet and looked down at her copybook.

It was our last day in primary school. They could keep their old secondary school, because I had somewhere altogether more interesting to go, a school far away from this convent and all these women in black. The other girls in the class smiled nervously at me, but nobody dared say anything. They all stood up again as Sister Evangelist left the room. I remained seated wondering about how nuns made up their minds about things. Weren't they supposed to be God' representatives on earth?

That was the first summer I didn't go down to Wexford.

My friendship with Joan and Dolores ended then too. Nothing really happened—we didn't fall out or anything like that. We just went our separate ways and developed friendships with different girls. Our growing interests swept us to different places.

I was twelve years of age now, almost a teenager. Instead of playing games in back gardens and sheds, my new interest was in going to the pictures with my big sister Peg to watch big people acting in stories. Just how did films get made? Did someone follow you around with a big camera and wait until you said something interesting? Or wait until something exciting happened? I wasn't really sure.

It was only when I saw a film with Jacqueline Ryan, the young girl star, that I realised there was such a thing as 'acting'. People pretending to be people they weren't. That was what I wanted to do now—pretend to be other people.

Jacqueline Ryan had gone to St Louis' secondary school in Rathmines, just a few minutes' walk from where I lived. If she could get into films, then so could I. I didn't tell anyone about my thoughts. They would only laugh and make fun of me.

The name of Jacqueline Ryan's film was actually *Jacqueline*. It was set in Belfast and told the story of a young girl's boozy father who loses his job in the shipyards and tries to pull himself back up in the world. It was in a long line of Irish 'shenanigans' sort of films and fairly typical of those set in Ireland at the time. There was drinking, dancing and singing, and rows over religion and politics, with a little love thrown in to spice it up. Stalwarts like Noel Purcell and Marie Keane had main roles. But all that passed over my head then, of course. All I thought about was the thrill of having a film called after you! Could there ever be a film called *Phyl*, I wondered?

> *Many years later a film called* Philomena *was made, and that is the name on my birth certificate. I wasn't to know then that my name wouldn't be the only thing I had in common with the main character.*

During that summer, I was wandering around town with my new friends when I noticed a big poster for the film *Jacqueline* in a shop window in Abbey Street. I pressed my face up against the pane, ignoring the shouts of my friends to hurry up. I let them walk on. Jacqueline Ryan was around the same age as me. She had a nice face and a fringe too. My hair was too curly to have a fringe. Jacqueline's hair was fair and mine was dark. We were the same height.

I realised, as I gazed through the window, that this was no ordinary shop. Located between the China Showrooms and Wynn's Hotel, it was run by Film Distributors, and the posters were there to advertise their business. Another poster I spotted read 'Ardmore Studios in Bray' in big, colourful letters. This must mean that films were made in Ireland, because I knew Bray. There was a big hill there called Bray Head, an amusement arcade and lots of seaside B&Bs.

My mind was made up. I memorised the number of the shop and decided to write a letter when I got home.

It was my first time to write a letter to someone I didn't know. To my great surprise, I received a reply within a week. It was the first time a letter addressed to me came through our letterbox. To my horror, however, my sister Mary had opened it and stumbled on my secret. How could she do that to me? The letter invited me to visit the film distributors' office when I was next passing. The man who had written the letter said that we could talk about my plans. It might seem odd these days, but I am still grateful to that man—whoever he was—who had the generosity to answer the letter of a twelve-year-old girl living in a fantasy world.

My little bubble was well and truly burst by my sister. She probably thought that she was helping me. I saw it as a betrayal of my privacy. I ignored the invitation to become another Jacqueline Ryan and buried that particular dream.

6. SANDYMOUNT HIGH

In September 1957 I began my secondary education in Sandymount High School. It was one of the few co-educational schools in Dublin. The school's liberal approach to education, with no emphasis on religion, marked it out as a sort of glamorous place to attend.

The school was founded in 1947 by Patrick Cannon and his wife Eileen. It consisted of a few classrooms behind the Cannon house in Herbert Road. To set up a new school, the Department of Education required a letter from the Archbishop of Dublin Archbishop. Patrick Cannon knew that the Catholic Archbishop, John Charles McQuaid, would never give him such a letter, so he got what was required from the Church of Ireland Archbishop, satisfying the Department's rule. To counteract this new liberal approach to education, John Charles arranged for Marian College, a secondary school for boys managed by the Marist Brothers, to be established on the grounds beside Sandymount High.

Coming to Sandymount straight from a convent education was like leaving a monochrome world and suddenly being immersed in a sea of colour. Our uniform was primrose yellow and blue. Primrose, as a common colour, was new to me. Instead of the teachers wearing black habits with rosary beads swinging from their waists, they wore academic gowns that ballooned behind them as they walked from class to class. The teachers were exotic creatures to us convent-bred students.

Charles Mitchell, Ireland's first television newsreader, taught us elocution.

A very young Bríd Rodgers, who was later to became a politician with the SDLP in Northern Ireland, taught us Irish and French. I loved the sound of her voice, particularly when she spoke in French. Ruth and Susan Browne, daughters of Dr Noel Browne, the social and political campaigner and a champion in the fight against TB, were students there during my time, as was the historian and journalist Ruth Dudley Edwards.

Mrs Donaldson, one of my favourite teachers, introduced us to sport for the first time in our young lives. I remember one particularly fierce hockey match against the Masonic School, a boarding school for girls set in a redbrick building next to the RDS in Ballsbridge. The quaint concept of ladylike competition died a death that day as both sides went at it hammer and tongs.

Sandymount High used the continental system of education. Classes started at 8.30am and finished at 2pm A gang of us used to travel on the 18 bus and occupy the front rows of upstairs seats. We were a small community of young people who lived near each other and who kept each other company every day on the bus. On the way home, Betty Smith always took up the centre position, with her back to the front window, and entertained us with her uproarious renditions of her favourite Elvis song, *Blue Suede Shoes*. It all stopped when one day the bus came to a sudden halt at the top of Waterloo Road and the driver came rushing up the stairs and said, 'If yez don't stop banging over me head I'll bar the lot of yez.'

Years later, I heard that Betty had become a nun. I just hope her vocation didn't require her to publicly renounce her love of Elvis.

Jimmy (Tubby) Abel—later a very successful architect—lived a few doors up our road and he would entertain us by mimicking the voice of our Latin teacher. 'You're like a Christmas pudding. You're all mixed up,' he'd say. We were studying Latin and French for the first time now, and often mixed up the two vocabularies. Roddy O'Sullivan, a tall, handsome boy, used to sit quietly and watch all our carry-on from a polite distance. He went on to become a professor of dentistry in UCD. Where are they all now I wonder?

Nothing would keep me out of school, and every day spent there was a real joy. Students were listened to and my English essays were read out to the class. This was the first time in my life that I was regularly praised, an experience I grew to like. To praise a child then wasn't the done thing. It was believed that you would give them a 'big head', making them feel they were better than their peers. I never felt better than anyone else. In Sandymount High, I was simply learning to feel just as valued as the next student. At the end of first year, Noel Browne was invited to present the prizes. I was presented with a book for coming first in my class. My confidence was growing now, and I felt that I was really starting to think for myself.

My father was proud of my achievements, though he didn't tell me so himself. I only learned about it years later, after his death, when one of his work colleagues told me that he was always talking about me. Only then did I realise how hard he had worked to find the money to pay my fees. He never complained about it. He had a private press on the wall that he called his Sheriff's Office. At the beginning of each term, he would open it with great ceremony and take out the required money to cover my school fees. Years later too, I thought about the poems and ballads he had written that were locked away in that press, and wondered how his life would have been had he had the opportunity to develop his talents. Like so many of his generation, his private dreams were locked away.

When I got home from school each day the house was empty, except, of course, for my mother. My sisters and brothers had already finished their lunch and returned to school or work. It was the first time in my life that I had my mother all to myself. I always wished that she would sit down and talk to me, but she never did. She always seemed to be busy. One lunchtime I rushed home to tell my mother that I had been chosen for the debating team. I was over the moon about it. But I never got to tell her that day, because right there, sitting at the lunch table in my place, was our next-door neighbour.

My mother stretched out her hand as though she were introducing an honoured guest. 'Mr Halpin will be here for lunch during his weekdays, from now on.'

Mr Halpin's mouth melded into a watery smile. Time hadn't mellowed the glassy-eyed stare.

I was sure he could see the horror etched into my face. I forced a smile and said, 'Hello Mr Halpin.'

He carried on eating, cutting up his meat as though the food on the plate was struggling to escape his knife and fork. My mother put down my plate in front of me and carried on talking to him. And now I had one more thing to worry about: Mr Halpin would be coming into our house every day, during my lunchtime, now that his wife had died.

My mother leaned across the table. 'Would you like another slice of apple tart, Mr Halpin?'

'No thank you, Missus. You have me spoilt. I won't be able to do a spot of work after this big meal.'

Not that he ever did do a spot of work. All he did was stand at the gates of a cemetery watching people go in and out. His biggest task was to ring the bell at the end of the day, then lock the gates to keep out the rest of the world above ground. It was his wife who had always done all the work: early morning shifts in Trinity College, cleaning the place for the students, then home to cook lunch for 'My Jim.'

My three years in Sandymount High School came to an end after my Intermediate Certificate. My mother felt I could be more usefully educated in a secretarial college, where I could learn the skills that would guarantee me employment. My brother Thomas, three years younger than me attended Sandymount High too, and went on to complete the Leaving Certificate, while another brother Eamonn was sent to the local technical school. Funds from my father's Sheriff's Office were running low.

7. AER LINGUS

Armed with the qualifications of a good shorthand and typing certificate, gained from the O'Donnell Commercial College in Rathmines, I sat the Aer Lingus public exam. The prospect of earning my own money was very attractive to me, as was the opportunity to be able to contribute to our household.

I passed the test. The airport was like a village back then, with a bow-shaped terminal building at its centre and a few administrative offices sprinkled here and there, and two canteens to feed the varied and colourful employees.

The office I worked in was a bit like a playground, but there was a pay packet at the end of each week. For many of us, it was our first real job. Typing invoices for incoming cargo certainly wasn't taxing work. The large office space with eight typists and more than twenty male clerks was a busy place, operating from 7am to 10pm with rostered shifts.

An Aer Lingus van picked me up from home at 6.30am and I joined the other early morning crew on the drive out to the airport. I loved travelling in the same van as the air hostesses and pilots in their immaculate uniforms and I took pleasure in studying these girls, all a bit older than me, watching them apply their make-up from their fancy vanity cases. Some day I would wear make-up. But not just yet. Maybe when I turned nineteen. Maybe, some day, I would apply to become an air hostess and travel around the world. An Aer Lingus air hostess was something to be back then. Men boasted that their friends were married to one.

My typing job was a very mechanical operation, demanding no great intellectual application. There was plenty of time for chat with the other typists and the clerks who hovered around our desks, collecting the invoices as they were typed. Part of the typists' duties was to phone the new television station, Telefís Éireann, when a fresh newsreel arrived in on a plane. Phoning the station made us feel important, being the first to inform them of the arrival of news from abroad.

We sat on either side of a long table churning out invoices. At the head of the table sat a clerk who was in charge of the manifest sheets from the incoming flights. The clerks would wheel a trolley to the typing area, collect the invoices and then transport them to another section of the big office for further processing. The trolley was almost like a member of the staff, whizzing up and down the office all day with its cargo of invoices. The night staff had other uses for this trolley, though, as I would soon learn.

Though it was a real job, it wasn't like a really serious one for us girls, because all we seemed to do all day was laugh and chat about what we had done the night before. About which programmes we had seen on the new television station and so on. The male staff were mostly young, from all over Ireland, and they took much delight in teasing and showing off in front of the captive audience in the typing pool. We were like an extended family, I suppose.

We ate together in the staff canteen along with all the airport workers, air hostesses, pilots and maintenance men. Each section had their own eating areas. Although there was, as you would expect, a pecking order, we all queued up together and ate from the same menu. When five o'clock came the evening staff would walk across the airport grounds, past the main terminal building to the canteen, to have a leisurely meal. The general chat would range from office business to books read to what was on in the cinema and on television. One man, Dan Doyle, was working his way through all of Charles Dickens's novels. We called him Dan Dickens. He was the reason I took out *Great Expectations* from Rathmines library.

One evening when I was the only typist on the late shift, a clerk called Jim, always a bit of a ringleader when it came to office antics, sidled over to my desk with the trolley and asked me if I had finished typing the invoices. Before I could gather my thoughts, he hoisted me up and set me down on the trolley. Then, with the help of the other men, he pulled up my skirt to reveal the soft part of my thigh, between the top of my nylon stockings and suspender belt. Jim then held a rubber stamp aloft to 'christen me'.

'You are now officially one of our team!'

For some inexplicable reason this experience didn't come as a shock to me, nor did it seem like a sexual assault. I think at some level I must have known previously about it. This ritual, it transpired, was what every new girl had to endure. It was simply accepted as part of the nighttime activity, and nobody ever raised an eyebrow about it.

What wasn't talked about at all was what might happen on the drive from the airport into the city after night duty. It certainly wasn't a regular occurrence, but it was a feature of the period in Ireland when girls didn't know how to respond or didn't have the vocabulary to express their anger.

One night, the supervisor gave me and another clerk a lift back into town. I was sitting on the back seat beside a young clerk. At one stage, I felt his hand making its way towards my panties while I listened studiously to what the driver was saying. I pushed the hand away immediately, as if I were swatting a fly. I didn't want to shout at the clerk because I didn't want to show him up in front of the supervisor. Neither did I want to let the supervisor think that I would condone such behaviour.

The next day, when the same clerk came to my desk to collect invoices, it was as if nothing at all had happened. I told nobody about this event.

8. LOVE-STRUCK

The next couple of years passed without much ado. I continued living at home, the Aer Lingus staff bus swinging by on my early morning shifts to pick me up. Then my two older sisters got married. My parents had a sense that some of the fledglings were officially flying the nest. I watched it all from a casual, if content, distance. I was happy for my sisters, of course, but the whole wedding idea didn't attract me. Nor was I pining for liberation from the family nest. However, when my birthdays came and went, I began to be restless for some new interest in life—and it didn't have much to do with settling down to suburban bliss and babies. I was the girl in that song, 'I never will marry, I'll be no man's wife, I'll always stay single, all the days of my life.'

A poster for actors on the staff noticeboard caught my eye. The Aer Lingus Musical and Dramatic Society was inviting people to attend auditions for *Our Town*, by Thornton Wilder. The director cast me in a small part, speaking only one line. A new world opened up and a whole new cast of people emerged into my life. After rehearsals in the head office of Aer Lingus in O'Connell Street, we would go to the Rainbow Cafe for tea or ice-cream.

One night, a boy called Terry asked me if he could leave me home. It was well past midnight and the house was in darkness so we went around to the back. Terry followed me into the porch and started clowning around. Then he suddenly went quiet and kissed me and told me that he fancied me. I didn't know what to say.

Just at that moment a door opened and my mother appeared in a long white nightdress.

'Good evening, Lady Macbeth,' Terry proclaimed. 'I have delivered your daughter home safely.' The attitude was a little cheeky, when I think about it now. But my mother made no reply, good, bad or indifferent. I scuttled inside and closed the door tightly after me.

The tone over breakfast the next morning was curt. 'When was the last time you were at confession, young lady?'

I turned away from her and said nothing. Silence was becoming my strong suit now, more and more.

'You can't have been up to any good with that young man in the dark.'

I had never had a boyfriend, even though I had been to several 'hops'—dances in Dublin's tennis and rugby clubs. My first date never happened either, because, on the way to meet him, I got cold feet and turned home rather than appear at the appointed place. In relation to men, I was a blank page.

I met Terry again in Vaughan's pub in Terenure. This time he told me he wouldn't run the risk of meeting Lady Macbeth again. He would have me home before midnight.

The last night of rehearsals for *Our Town* was a memorable one for reasons that didn't have much to do with Thornton Wilder. We were all sitting around the table listening to the sombre voice of Maurice O'Doherty reading the six o'clock television bulletin, when he announced that some breaking news had just come in. The sallow, stern face on the black and white screen fell silent. It took him a moment to read the script as he was visibly affected by its content. 'President Kennedy has been shot in Dallas, Texas...assassinated.'

It was Friday, November 22, 1963. In Ireland, John F Kennedy was spoken of in the same reverent tone as the Pope. Many houses had a standard triad of photos on their walls: JFK, the Pope and the Sacred Heart. These three were the icons of many childhoods. The assassination was a punctuation mark in many lives.

Around that time, my friend Claire asked me to accompany her to a play in town. Claire was a glamorous person and really good company. My brothers used to call her 'Marilyn Monroe.' I jumped at the chance. This was in a real theatre, the Unicorn Theatre, in the basement of a Georgian house in North Great George's Street, near O'Connell Street. It had a proper stage and raked seating. Claire's friend had quite a big part in the play.

I was getting used to going into town at night after the Aer Lingus rehearsals in O'Connell Street. Claire had no real interest in theatre, but she did have an interest in men. When we were sitting in the theatre, waiting for the curtains to open, I felt as if I had arrived at a place of peace, a place where I felt at home. But also a place tinged with excitement. The anticipation of waiting for the red velvet curtain to open was like that of a child on Christmas morning, waiting to discover what marvel Santa had delivered. I was happy enough to be in the audience, but I really wanted to find out what went on behind the curtain.

When the play was over, Claire turned to me. 'Bill said to wait for him.'

It wasn't long before he came out to the front of the theatre. 'Hello, darling. Sorry for the delay, I had to take off my greasepaint.'

He acknowledged my presence with a wink, and, putting his arm around Claire's shoulder, said, 'C'mon girls, let's go for a drink.'

The Metro pub was around the corner on Parnell Street, only a few minutes' walk away. This was new territory for me and I was beginning to feel like a grown-up now, waiting to see what the next stage of life had to show me. Claire was full of life and full of confidence, something to do with being an only child, I secretly suspected, with being listened to by her parents because there was time and space. Her clothes were always the latest fashion, and to add to all these gifts, she was blonde. She always wore make-up and perfume. Beside her, I felt like her dowdy sister. And Claire sparkled most of all in the company of men.

The cast of the play was already standing at the bar drinking. Claire perched herself on a high stool facing Bill. I sat on the only empty stool, facing into the crowd. It was a good position to take it all in at a safe distance. The hum of male voices caught my ear now. They were discussing how Shakespeare could enter the female psyche. I wasn't altogether sure what 'psyche' meant but I had a notion it was something to do with desire or maybe emotions. *Romeo and Juliet* was mentioned. One voice spoke with more authority than the rest of the speakers. A strong, stentorian sort of voice, very sure of itself. I didn't have to strain to hear it. 'Love can blossom at any age.'

I felt the voice coming nearer to me. I saw Claire turning towards its source and disengaging from Bill. Her face lit up. The man with the golden voice looked at Claire for a moment and then at me. 'I prefer dark-haired beauties.' His voice resonated with something deep inside me, as if a silk blanket had brushed over my skin.

'Brian. I'm Brian.' He extended his hand and I took it. He was older than me, a real man, I thought, not like the boys I worked with. Not like my brothers either. This fellow was like no one I had ever met before. He was like a film star. But I couldn't think which one exactly, I was so flustered. 'You are the very girl I'm looking for!'

Claire was dumbstruck and turned back to Bill.

'What did you think of the play?' Brian's hazel eyes held me in a clinch. He didn't bother waiting for my reply. 'Have you any acting experience?'

I told him about my part in *Our Town*. I didn't reveal that I had only one line.

He fixed his dark-rimmed glasses on his nose and pushed nearer to me, as if he was looking for some evidence of acting ability in my face. I could feel a blush stealing over my cheeks. He glanced at his watch then turned back to me and smiled. 'Look, come to my auditions next week. Our next production is J B Keane's *The Highest House on the Mountain*.'

My excitement was really ratcheting up now.

When I think back to that moment, the word 'ingénue' comes to mind. The dictionary definition is 'a naive or artless young woman.' Without being too hard on myself—I was very young, after all—it is an accurate description of the girl I was at that time.

My inexperience showed, especially when it came to rehearsals. When Brian cast me as the young lead, I was initially lost. I don't remember any analysis of my character or stagecraft. What I do remember is the director's emphasis on blocking out the actors' moves on the stage and writing the exits and entrances on my script.

After rehearsals, the entire cast went around the corner to the Metro. It never occurred to me to ask for help, or if it did, I wouldn't have known what to ask for. I was lost and confused, and the young man who played my new husband seemed a bit lost too. After a few pints in the pub, he would expound on the Ingmar Bergman film he had seen or the book he had been reading, with no reference to the play we had been in. It was all a bit disconnected.

One night he walked me to my bus stop on Burgh Quay. As my bus came to the stop, he pulled me towards him and kissed me on the cheek. 'I'm beginning to fall for you.'

Now, there was only one person I was falling for, and that was the director, whose voice was like a warm hug every time he spoke. His parting words, as I left the pub earlier, were still tingling in my head. 'Come here to me, pet.' He held my hand and then kissed it. 'Be a good girl now and learn your lines before the dress rehearsal.'

When I arrived at the theatre on opening night, he had left a message written with red lipstick on the mirror over my space in the dressing room. 'Break a leg. I'll see you after the show.'

But he didn't turn up. I discovered that on the same night, at the Damer Theatre in St Stephen's Green, he was writing exactly the same message on the dressing room mirror of another ingénue. But this time the message was *as Gaeilge* as was the play, *An Giall,* the original Irish-language version of Brendan Behan's *The Hostage.*

In the J B Keane play, I started to slowly find a way into the character of the new wife as she joined her husband's dysfunctional family, the Bannons. Not only was my character from a different country, but the Bannon family were all strangers to her, except for the man she had married. She was faced with the problem of learning how to survive and how to be accepted. She would balance this with a stubborn refusal to change her personality to fit into this new way of life.

My character's dilemma resonated with my own life at that point. Towards the middle of the run, Brian, came to see the play. After the curtain call, he appeared in the dressing room to talk to the cast. We all listened to his words carefully, both the praise and the criticism. Then we headed for the door. We had all, by this stage, become used to taking off our make-up and changing into our day clothes fast enough to make it to the Metro before closing time.

Brian, walked behind me on the way out. I heard him say to one of the actors, 'Oh, damn it! I've left my bag behind me at the Damer.' He hesitated and rummaged in his pockets as if looking for something. 'Look, I'll see you all on the last night. Slán.' When I turned to say good night, he caught me by the hand firmly and said, 'You're coming with me. I want to talk to you.'

My stage husband stood nearby for a moment, waiting to see if I would follow. This moment was the real-life cliffhanger. Would I dive or swim on? Before I knew it, I was sitting in the front seat of Brian's car. 'Sorry about the opening night, pet. I had to be with the cast of *An Giall*, up in the Damer. There were technical problems.'

He parked his car on St Stephen's Green. Then, instead of walking towards the Damer theatre to pick up his bag, he took my hand and led me towards the Winter Garden Palace pub on the corner. High-pitched voices and smoky fumes spilled out as he opened the door. This place was much bigger than the Metro and there were far more people inside. Sitting on the floor in the corner I could see a little group of people, all of them shouting out Brian's name. One of them held up his bag and said something in Irish. The young girl he greeted as Neasa patted the space beside her. She gave him an order in Irish that signalled 'Sit beside me!' She didn't look at me at all. It was as if I wasn't there.

When Brian was ordering our drinks, the group continued to speak in Irish. I was really beginning to feel how it was for my character in *The Highest House on the Mountain* in real life now—to be with a group of people, or a family like the Bannons, and not to be able to join in the conversation. It was a strange feeling, and my mind wandered away to the art on the wall, the pictures of lakes and woodlands. I thought of all the paintings that my father had done on other people's walls. Of what my mother might say, if she saw me here with a glass of Smithwick's in one hand and a cigarette in the other as I sat beside a group of people speaking Irish and listening to every word coming out of the director's beautiful mouth.

When last orders were shouted, Neasa whispered something in Brian's ear. She looked over at me with a mock serious face and said, 'I suppose you're waiting for the translation?'

I was annoyed at myself for going red. Then Brian came to my rescue, explaining all about the history of the drama. I wasn't worried about the translation of the play, of course. I just wanted the translation of whatever Neasa was whispering in my lovely director's ear.

We were the last to leave the pub and the last bus was well gone. Brian said he would drive me home, even though he lived on the north side of the city and I lived on the south side. 'I won't see you until Saturday, pet. This gang are closing tomorrow night.' He pulled me towards him and softly kissed me on the lips before I got out of the car.

My mother was waiting up for me when I tiptoed through the hall door. 'And what kept you out till this hour? You can't have been up to anything good.'

I muttered something about a meeting after the play and that I had missed the last bus. But she wasn't buying that version of events. Maybe she sensed there was something new possessing her daughter. That she was adrift and in danger, more than her daughter herself knew.

Brian came to the closing night of *The Highest House on the Mountain*. I was thankful that I couldn't see him from the stage but I could hear his laugh, even though there were very few moments of fun in the play. At the curtain call, he stood up from his back row seat and blew a kiss in my direction. At least, I thought it was a kiss for me. But when I looked around at the rest of the cast, I realised they were all looking at him too.

The relief of knowing that I would never again have to inhabit the role of the unfortunate woman in the play made me giddy. It was like shedding a load that had weighed me down for weeks. There was an air of celebration in the dressing room too. Relief that we had come through the storm and arrived safely home.

'Last out turns off the lights,' shouted my stage husband. Then the tall figure of Brian appeared. 'Bravo! You did it. I'll turn out the lights and lock up. See you all around the corner.' He threw me another kiss.

I was sitting on a bar stool talking to Claire, who had come to see the play, when he arrived in a while later. He didn't come over. His presence brought a sort of comfort, though, even from a distance. It was near closing time when he finally joined our little group. 'Bob has invited us all back to his flat.' Bob, our stage manager, lived a few minutes away at the other end of Parnell Street.

Claire wanted to know if she and Bill could come too. Then she changed her mind because Bill said he wanted to go to Groome's, the late-night bar around the corner opposite the Gate Theatre. Brian looked over at me and said, 'Don't worry about your last bus. I'll give you a lift home.' When he placed his hand on the small of my back, I was undone right away. I knew I just had to go with him. Some of the cast bought bottles to continue drinking, but I had no interest in alcohol then.

We all crowded into Bob's sparsely furnished room. Most people sat on the floor, but Brian, claiming the only armchair, pulled me towards him and sat me on his knee. I had never sat on a man's knee before. Well, not as an adult anyway. Only Mr Halpin's, and that doesn't count.

The electricity meter had to be fed coins, and as nobody bothered to do so, the light soon disappeared. Only the weak glow from the Super Ser gas heater saved the room from total darkness. It was cold now and I felt a shudder down my back. Brian pulled me closer to him. I felt a comfort from the warmth of his body. Words were flying around the room at a great rate, but Brian's sonorous voice was the only one I was listening to.

It was getting late. I was worried about what my parents would think of me arriving home at an even later time than before. I made an attempt to move but Brian pulled me towards him. I could feel a swelling movement coming from his lap and his fingers working their way stealthily toward my undergarments. Shock and desire battled against each other, but only for a second before I registered what was actually happening. I didn't want to stand up for fear of exposing his opened fly. I turned to him and whispered that I wanted to go to the toilet, giving him time to compose himself and, just as importantly, giving me time to protect my reputation.

It was shortly after this that I realised Brian was a married man with children, but such details were far from my head at the time. I was incapable of extricating myself; the fire of passion was burning, and I was out of control. Brian was standing up when I returned. It was as if nothing had happened between us. He spoke to the room as if addressing a theatre audience. 'Now, let's take this young girl home.' And then we left.

9. LONDON

My life with Brian, even though we never actually lived together, carried on apace. I was consumed with passion for this man I hadn't known a year before. There were all sorts of trysts and nights of love and longing. One night I remember him stopping the car suddenly to visit a chemist shop around the corner from the Abbey Theatre on Eden Quay. When he came back he said, 'Medicine for the little one, he's not well.' And still I didn't comprehend that this man had a family, a family that didn't exist in my world. Another night as we sat in the Metropole cinema watching *Doctor Zhivago*, Brian turned to kiss me and said, 'That's us, consumed by passion.' Brian, at that moment in my eyes was a bit like Omar Sharif, and I was lost in the story of the film and in our own story. As we were leaving the cinema a friend of Brian's approached us and said, 'I see you are in new company these days.' At the time I didn't understand the significance of the comment. He was sitting near us in the cinema and must have seen Brian kissing me.

Our relationship shuttled along frantically, with us grabbing time together whenever circumstances allowed. If discretion was part of our dating, caution certainly wasn't common currency between us. If either of us thought about the consequences, fate didn't pay much heed to our worries. It wouldn't take long before the price of desire was written out on my body. The sum of umpteen clandestine nights in his car, listening to his dulcet tones, letting his seductive words infiltrate my entire world, my entire being.

One night, as we were parked in the Phoenix Park, a garda tapped the car window. We were both at a fairly advanced state of undress. Brian wound down the window slowly, looking out at the police uniform.

'Is that a young girl you have with you there, sir? I think it's time you took her home.'

For once, the loquacious Brian was lost for words. He tidied himself up quickly and turned the key in the ignition without saying a word. But I just had to speak. I had to say my piece. 'God wouldn't have made us this way if it was a crime.'

Though the passion we felt for each other was powerful and real, I certainly wasn't seeing reality—or allowing myself to. I desperately needed him to say something in the situation with the garda to assure me of his feelings. Instead, he behaved as if he had been caught in an act he was ashamed of. The real point of my indignation was that I wasn't ashamed of my desire for the man I adored.

In February 1967, I left home, and Aer Lingus. My mother thought I was foolish to be giving up a good pensionable job. I told her, by way of an explanation, that I wanted to travel. That, after London, I would go to Paris to improve my French, and that I had a job lined up in Paris. But if my suitcase held all my worldly possessions, the pack of lies I carried in myself was a far heavier burden.

My destination was St Philomena's, a hostel in Euston Square in London run by nuns. Nobody in my family noticed that I was five months pregnant, even though a ladder in my stockings would have been a topic of conversation and criticism. A friend from Aer Lingus who did notice my body change went so far as to tell me that the extra weight I was carrying didn't suit me. That I should try dieting.

In reality, my immediate future had been mapped out for me by a German doctor on the north side of the city, who confirmed my pregnancy. I didn't dare visit a doctor on the south side. She was very practical, setting out all the steps that would take me to London and then return later to give birth anonymously in St Patrick's Mother and Baby Home on the Navan Road in Dublin.

Anonymous to everybody, that is, except to the baby's father.

When I told Brian I was pregnant, his first reaction was, 'Are you sure I'm the father?' How could he ask me this when he knew that he was the first man I had made love with. He knew that there was nobody else in my life. At one stage he told me that a friend of his had just qualified as a doctor and that he could ask him about the possibility of arranging an abortion for me. Abortion was totally unacceptable morally and legally at that time; the story of the back-street abortionist Nurse Cadden who had been convicted of murder was still fresh in people's minds. I couldn't consider such a procedure.

Before I left Dublin, Brian and I spent a last night together in a hotel in Lucan. He had told his wife that he was travelling up north to adjudicate at a drama festival. It was the first time we had actually slept in a bed together. The next morning he drove me home. 'When you come back we will talk about things.' That was all he said when we parted. I didn't really know what he meant then, nor did I know how I felt either. It was as if I were living in someone else's world now, and didn't know where I was going.

Euston Square wasn't exactly the most salubrious of London locations. From the Thirties onwards it was one of the places you could find those unfortunate Irish who had fled their failed country and ended up sleeping on park benches. It was as if they had just stumbled off the train from Holyhead, straight to a park bench and never left it. I felt a terrible twinge of pity whenever I spotted one of them, homeless and hopeless, trying to preserve what little dignity was left to them.

St Philomena's hostel, right in the centre of that world, was where young women came to get a safe head-start before striking out for their own accommodation. The nuns managed the hostel very efficiently, and the cost was low.

A young nun showed me to the room I was to occupy for the next few weeks. Three single beds filled the space, and mine was the one beside the window. Bedside lockers separated the beds. The dark decor was all that I could take in when I entered the room: dark-brown wallpaper with orange dots and heavy curtains just a paler shade of mud and dust.

'You will be sharing the room with two other girls. Leave your case there and let me show you where the toilets and bathrooms are.'

I followed the nun along a grey passageway, where girls of all ages passed by with towels around their heads. It was like a boarding school for grown-ups, where the girls were free during the day, but a ten o'clock curfew was the immovable rule.

This accommodation would be my bolthole for a few weeks. I became friendly with my two room-mates. Helen was twenty-two, the same age as myself, and had recently arrived from Scotland. She was working in Marks & Spencer on Oxford Street. Helen was a serious girl who rarely smiled, but I liked her all the same. There was something very fragile about her.

The other girl, Mayumi, was Japanese, and she smiled all the time. I had never met a person from Japan before, but I did have a huge appreciation of what little I had seen of Japanese art. When Mayumi was leaving to return to her home in Tokyo, she gave me a beautiful pair of pyjamas that her grandmother had made for the cold English climate. She liked to practise her English with us before going asleep. Often she would question us about what she had learned in class that day. It was difficult for her to distinguish the L sound from the R sound so myself and Helen diplomatically used a jingle to help her with her pronunciation:

Run rabbit, run rabbit,
Run, run, run.

Then we would all settle down to sleep. Sometimes Mayumi would ask me about phrases and parts of grammar. In school, we had been well grounded in English grammar. Every sentence was parsed, word by word, so I loved answering her questions.

Irish grammar was an entirely different story. Brian was a fluent Irish speaker and was intolerant of bad pronunciation or bad grammar. For that reason, I never attempted to speak in Irish in his presence for fear of being ridiculed. He freely admitted to being an intellectual snob in this regard. His only reference to my lack of the language was once during love making, when he said, 'It's a pity you can't make love *as Gaeilge*.'

I thought about him constantly now and wondered if he was thinking of me. The urge to connect with him was a constant ache, but I had no way of contacting him. The first long day in London stretched before me now. I knew that I needed to find work. But the need for a cigarette was far more urgent. Something to calm my nerves.

It didn't take me long to find a corner shop. It was like walking into a telephone booth, it was so tiny. The unsmiling woman behind the counter peered over her glasses at me. 'Yes?'

'Ten Players Number Six, please.'

She looked at me as if I was speaking a foreign language. I was shocked that she couldn't understand.

'Sorry, luv, what ya saying?'

A young man entered the shop at that moment. She made a funny face and then looked over my shoulder at her next customer. A confusion of embarrassment and shock flooded over me. I remember thinking to myself at that moment: you either imitate her English accent or you accentuate you own.

In Ireland, when a person returned home with an English accent after hardly a wet weekend away, it had always been a cause for ridicule. I spoke again, intent on keeping my accent. Slowly and clearly. 'Ten Players Number Six, please.'

It was at that precise moment I accepted that I was in a different country. And that I had to hold on to my identity, whatever that was.

That day, I walked around the area until I found an employment agency. I needed work because my financial situation wasn't good. However, my shorthand and typing skills were, and I was sure I could function in any office setting. The agency offered me a position in the typing pool at the Royal Bank of England on Threadneedle Street, starting the following Monday.

I left the hostel early on the Monday to be on time for my new job. The agency had told me that the bank was looking for a girl for perhaps two weeks or longer, and that I could walk from my hostel in Euston Square. They gave me a map of the area and marked out the route for me. I walked through the park opposite the hostel, noticing for the first time how the trees were on the verge of opening their buds. This new city would provide me with a glimmer of hope. All I really knew was that I was escaping from Dublin, and from Irish eyes. I was hiding my secret in a new city where nobody knew me or knew about my pregnancy.

A man stretched out on a park bench shouted over at me. I copped the Irish country accent immediately. How could anybody end up like that? What was his story? I quickened my pace until I spotted the spires of St Paul's and knew that I hadn't far to go.

A colourful kiosk on the side of the street caught my eye and I stopped to look at the newspapers and magazines. 'Ten Players Number Six, please.' The shopkeeper understood my request right away. Success. I sauntered on towards the bank.

The girls in the typing pool were friendly. It was a relief that I had to wear an office coat, which provided cover for my bump. It was a navy-blue nylon overall, a standard uniform for typists, and while it did conceal my secret, it proved a very hot camouflage during office hours. At that time, I was under the illusion that nobody noticed I was pregnant. But of course I was in a state of gross denial. I found English people very non-judgemental in comparison to the Irish. On my last day at the bank I was pleasantly taken aback when the girls presented me with a cake during our tea break and then gave me a beautiful Mary Quant make-up box. It was such a generous act and, looking back now, I'm sure that they all knew of my condition. But they never made me feel different to them.

A few weeks after arriving in the hostel, Helen, my roommate, approached me and said, 'I think we're both in the same boat.' It was only then that I really realised my condition was obvious.

Helen and I searched the letting agencies for somewhere to move on to. Within days, we found a flat in St John's Wood. An elderly Jewish landlady interviewed us. We spun her a convoluted yarn that she swallowed because we both knew that, in reality, our term of residency would be limited to our babies' due dates. Helen kept on her job in Marks & Spencer, but I was in need of another job. I felt now that office work would be out of the question. Then I saw an advertisement in the local shop window: *Cleaner wanted three mornings a week for light household duties*

I could handle that. The address was just down the road from where I was staying. The following day I headed there.

Peter Noble and his wife, a couple in their fifties, welcomed me into their house as though I were a long-lost friend. Peter was a writer and worked most days from home. His wife was an actress. The first day I arrived was the morning after a big party. All sorts of crockery and glassware and bowls of different shapes and colours were stacked high on the kitchen table. The rays of the sun hit the glass bowls and it was like a rainbow had landed in front of me. 'The troops were here last night,' Peter said.

His wife eyed me up quietly, wondering if I was up to the task, I suppose. I wasn't sure if she had already spotted my condition. 'I'll be back at lunchtime and we'll see then how you are getting on.' She kissed her husband and left for rehearsals.

'We had Cleo and Shirley here last night. They were trying out their new songs. Do you know them?' Peter's smiling face beamed at me. He couldn't have meant Cleo Laine and Shirley Bassey, could he? I knew them well because I was interested in jazz. I had been to Liberty Hall in Dublin with Brian to see Cleo Laine and Johnny Dankworth a few months before I got pregnant.

'Oh, yes,' I said.

Peter beamed at me again. I was in heaven here. I was about to wash the glasses, plates, cups and saucers that Cleo and Shirley had used the previous night. This was a new drama for me, with a new cast of characters. As I washed the dishes, Peter kept walking in and out of the kitchen to see how I was getting on.

'You're very young to be doing this sort of work, aren't you?'

A tenderness stole into his voice. The voice mellowed further. 'Take your time, darling. There's no rush. If you need me, I'm in my study.'

'Darling…' Nobody had every called me that before. Well, maybe Brian had, but I think he said 'pet' more than 'darling.' This felt good now. I felt like I was in a newly adopted home.

The click-clack of Peter's typewriter led me to his study which opened out onto an adjoining drawing room.

'I'm finished in the kitchen. What else can I do?'

He pointed to the ladder against the bookshelves. 'Those books up there haven't seen a duster in years.'

I could feel his eyes burning through me now as I climbed up the steps. The playfulness had gone from his voice. It had been replaced by a worried tone. He had clearly spotted my condition.

'Be very careful, darling.'

Peter chatted casually as I dusted. He told me he was in the middle of writing a script for BBC Radio. Although it was getting near the deadline date, he kept talking and asking me questions about myself. What had brought me to England? Where had I been living? What were my plans? His concern disarmed me at first, but then I felt free to tell him another lie as he listened intently. Listening in a way that I wasn't accustomed to.

'I've run away from my husband.'

His eyes opened wide. 'Oh, dear! Won't he be worried about you?'

I told him that my husband was involved in theatre and that, when he was working on a play, nothing else mattered. Peter asked me about the play. I told him that it was in the Irish language and was based on a book called *An Béal Bocht* by Flann O'Brien. I said that my husband had adapted it for the opening of a new theatre, the Peacock, below the Abbey Theatre. Those facts were true, except, of course, the part about him being my husband.

Peter pulled the sheet of paper out of his typewriter, threw it aside and put in a blank page. 'I'm now going to write a new play. A play about you, my little mysterious darling!'

On the third day when I came to the house, I overheard his wife talking in a loud voice. 'She's not what we want, Peter. She doesn't see what needs doing.'

When I was leaving after completing my few chores that day, Peter gave me an envelope with two weeks wages in it and said that he was sorry to lose me. He kissed me on the cheek and, I swear, I could see tears welling up in his deep blue eyes. Being let go didn't bother me at all really. I certainly didn't feel rejected. I thought to myself: all right, then, that's act one, scene one over and done with. Now, let's see where we go from here.

There was a parcel from Brian waiting for me when I got back to the flat. St Philomena's in Euston Square had forwarded it to my new address. There were two poetry books in the parcel and a short letter with his office address at the top of the page. I had never heard of the Czech poet Miroslav Holub, but I knew W B Yeats's poetry well.

Brian always wrote with a fountain pen. His handwriting was curved and elegant. 'Please let me know your return date. I miss you.' His handwriting was like a caress, and my whole body ached to see him.

I booked a flight to Belfast for the following week. Dublin Airport would be altogether too risky. There was the possibility that someone might see me and my secret would be revealed. I would be forever shamed as a fallen woman and a sinner. Only married people had the right to become pregnant. Unmarried pregnant women were viewed by society then as only slightly above prostitutes. My Scottish flatmate was also returning to her home to have her baby in secrecy, for the very same reason—the shame of pregnancy without a marriage licence.

The next few days went by in a whirl of dreaming and walking aimlessly around St John's Wood, hoping that I might bump into Peter Noble again. I would tell him that I had booked a flight. That I was going to be reunited with my husband. I would tell him that my husband was broken-hearted that I was so far away and that now he wanted to look after me and my baby, due in a few weeks' time.

One day, the baby began reminding me that it too had a life. The little kicks felt like sea waves flooding through me and I was overwhelmed with love for this, as yet, unknown, nameless child. Tears began to flow now. I felt like Anna Karenina, a woman on the brink of a big decision, with two impossible loves vying for my attention. I didn't realise, as I sobbed quietly to myself, that I was standing in front of a shop window. When I spotted the reflection of my ungainly shape, I was momentarily shocked. What would Brian think when he saw me? Would I ever regain my own body again?

A dress caught my eye: a vibrant shade of ochre and cream. I knew it would fit me after the baby was born. I would wear it for Brian when he came to visit me after the birth of our baby. And he would find me attractive again.

10. ST PATRICK'S

It was June 9, 1967, when I arrived in Belfast Airport. A lot of things had changed. Brian took my suitcase and told me that he had booked a room in a local hostel. I waited for him to put his arms around me but he didn't. I hid my disappointment, thinking that when we were alone later he would show me how pleased he was to see me. I could feel the tears welling up, but I didn't want to let them out. I had to keep strong.

When we sat in the car he looked at me and said, 'My wife knows.'

These words were uttered like a child saying that his mammy had found out the secret he was hiding.

'She found that pocketbook of Shakespearean sonnets you sent me.'

I couldn't speak.

'She read your inscription, *To my one and only love*.'

After receiving the poetry books from Brian, I wrote to thank him enclosing a miniature book of Shakespearian Sonnets to his office address, thinking nobody but Brian would see it.

The Belfast hostel was grotty and smelly, and I was hot and hungry. We slept on the lower bunk bed. After I had undressed, he turned his back to me and said simply, 'You'll need a good night's sleep.'

I lay awake half the night, longing for a caress. Longing for him to reach out for me, but all I could hear was his deep, laboured breathing. His dismissive words kept tumbling and crashing around in my head. I felt the baby moving all of a sudden, and I moved my hand gently over my stomach. I knew that I was alone now with this new life inside me.

We set off at first light the next morning in his white Volkswagen, registration, FIR 23. The word *fir* in the Irish language is the plural of *fear* and means 'men.') Brian, I now was beginning to realise, was not only a man living between two languages, but between two women. I trawled through my memory for some consoling words of his to hang on to. But the only sentence that came flooding back was the one he said when I told him that I was pregnant: 'Are you sure I'm the father?'

He didn't ask me about my time in London. In fact, he didn't ask much at all. And there was no mention of stopping for breakfast on the long drive to Dublin. It was as if he was in a hurry to get to the mother and baby home on the Navan Road in the desolate northern approach to the city.

I don't remember any of the conversation on that long journey, only that he stopped the car at some stage and said simply 'I need to stretch my legs.' He got out of the car. Then he came over to my side and opened the door. 'Get out for a minute, I have something to ask you.'

Could it be that he was leaving his wife and wanted to set up home with me and our baby? He was behaving strangely. He helped me out of the car. But there was no affection in the way that he touched me.

'My wife wants to know if you will come back to our house and have the baby there.'

It was like he had punched me in the stomach. My silence mutated into pure speechlessness. To consider such an invitation, even for a second, was unthinkable.

When I look back on that moment today, I have to acknowledge the generosity of someone who was prepared to have another woman living in her house—a woman not known to her and who was about to give birth to her husband's child. It was a magnanimous gesture.

But how would such a scenario have played out? Would it have turned into a modern version of 'Sister Brides, Sister Mothers,' the television programme based on the lives of several women living with the same man. Mind you, never at any stage did Brian tell me what he would have liked. Would he really have been happy for me to go to his home and live with his wife and children?

We drove in silence up the long gravel driveway to the big house on the Navan Road. Standing beside him at the huge hall door, I felt as if I was at the edge of a cliff, not knowing whether to jump or run.

Brian knocked on the door. A middle-aged, softly spoken nun answered. 'Come into the front room and I'll get Sister Joseph.'

The smell of lavender polish mixed with sizzling bacon wafted through the hall. It made me even dizzier with hunger. It suddenly dawned on me that I hadn't eaten anything since the day before, when I had a snack on the plane. A polished mahogany table filled the room. Portraits of archbishops and saints looked down on us from the space over the mantelpiece. Brian stood up when Sister Joseph entered the room. Brian was so tall, he hovered over her. I noticed now that he was all smiles. Smiles he hadn't shown me since my arrival.

'Sorry for the delay. I was having breakfast with our visiting priest.' The nun spoke directly to him and ignored me. She reminded me of Sister Evangelist from primary school.

'Will you consider keeping the baby when you get married?'she asked as she continued looking at Brian.

He didn't answer the question directly. 'I'm just very grateful that she can stay here with you, Sister, until the baby is born. Neither of our families know about the situation.'

In that moment I saw that he was a serious liar. He had given a false name for himself and for me. He registered me as Mary Hope. He was a convincing actor playing a very convincing role. As with acting, you have to convince yourself before you convince other people. Brian knew how to work an audience. I was beginning to believe, in an odd way, that I was part of some bigger drama that was being played out.

When Sister Joseph did eventually look in my direction, she said, 'You are very young, aren't you, dear?'

I wasn't that young. I was twenty-two, nearly twenty-three. But I didn't speak my thoughts, because I knew she wasn't finished talking.

'You are a lucky girl to have a fine man like this giving you support. I hope you realise that.' She reached for the bell on her table, shook it several times and then stood up. 'A sister will be here shortly to take you to your room.' Before leaving she smiled at Brian then disappeared out the door.

A moment later, Sister Lawrence appeared, a rosy-cheeked little nun. Brian shook hands with her, then turned to me. 'I'm sorry, pet, that it has to be this way.' He sighed at me as he left the house. Then Sister Lawrence nodded to me and brought me to my room.

It was a big surprise to me to discover that my sleeping area was separate from the other bunk beds in the dormitory—a private space with its own door. I thought it might have been originally designed for the nun on duty, but I didn't question it at the time.

The nursery was right beside the dormitory. At night I could hear the babies crying. Their cries were a source of comfort to me, as I was able to join in their chorus. Over the following weeks, I started missing Brian terribly, despite his behaviour when we had last met. I was disappointed that I hadn't heard from him. The Navan Road house felt strange and alien to me. For the first few days, it was as if I had crash-landed into some unknown territory and I was waiting for my man to rescue me. I wanted him to make everything right. But I had no idea how he would or could do that.

I went about in a haze of numbness. Then I met Emer, and she invited me to join her during her night duty hours. Before becoming pregnant she had been a student nurse. Her baby boy was now two weeks old and she was delighted to be on night duty in the nursery where she could be near him. The door into the nursery was beside my room, and at night I would go in to talk to her. She told me that the father of her child was a well-known ballad singer. He was also a married man.

Many years later, I heard him on the radio talking about his wife. He said she was the love of his life. Back then, Emer thought that she was.

She took me on a tour of the nursery. It was a huge room, as big as an acre of land, with white cots dotted in rows. Lines of them filled the space like drills of white unopened flower buds, lines of produce waiting to be claimed. The whole area was like a big baby farm with a constant line of incoming babies waiting for a new owner. Each cot was labelled with the name, weight and date of birth of the baby.

One night when we were chatting and laughing, Emer said, 'Soon your little one will be in one of these cots.' That was the moment I finally accepted that Brian wasn't going to rescue me. That I was alone.

A number of girls had recently given birth. Others, like me, were counting the days for their babies to be born. As reality began to sink in, I made up my mind to stay calm in the face of everything. The girls around me were from all over Ireland, all different ages. The youngest, a girl of thirteen, was a child who never spoke. We all minded her and fussed over her, and sometimes we even got her to laugh. Then one day we discovered that she had disappeared. We were later told that she had been taken away to a city hospital for the birth of her baby.

The oldest of us was in her forties. She was waiting for her farmer boyfriend to come and collect her after the birth of her child. We listened to her politely, knowing well that he would never show up.

'It's his busiest time of year on the farm,' she said when anyone asked her when he was coming. Next week, he'll be here when the work is finished.'

We would see her walking towards the front gate watching out for his car. That poor woman was living a dream, just like I was.

At night we would congregate in the kitchen and listen to music and tell jokes. We were like girls in a boarding school. Our main concern was to have our babies adopted so that we could walk out of St Patrick's as free agents, ready to start our lives all over again. That was the sort of mental bubble we were trapped in—the bubble that kept us sane.

One day I was called by the nun on duty to say that there was a visitor for me in the visitor's parlour.

At last, it's Brian! He's come to rescue me, I thought as I rushed up to the parlour. I opened the door to Gerry, a man I hardly knew. He worked in Harry Moore's, the radio and gramophone shop in Dawson Street, with my friend Claire. She had told him where I was.

He looked straight at me. 'Will you marry me, Phyl?'

This question landed on me like a bombshell. Gerry carried on. 'You can keep your baby and we can be the parents.' I had only met Gerry a few times and I liked him. But not in the way that I felt about Brian. I had to say no.

> *When I think of his generosity today, I am filled with gratitude for the courage that it took for this man to attempt to rescue me from the mother and baby home. I tried to make contact with him, to thank him, later, but I couldn't trace his whereabouts.*

The only people outside of St Patrick's I saw now were the priests and the visiting doctor. Although we went to mass every Sunday, I only remember visiting the doctor once. He weighed me and took my blood pressure without as much as looking at my face or uttering a word.

Details of my time in St Patrick's are a blur to me. But the days I spent with my baby girl can never be erased. It was a long labour—over eighteen hours. I remember that it was a sunny afternoon. I was put lying on what seemed like a table, in what I think was a kitchen, facing out onto a big field with a few apple saplings relieving the emptiness.

There were no curtains on the window. I could hear girls crying out in other parts of what must have been the delivery area. I couldn't make out where they were. I was in a separate or temporary section. I remember seeing a big broad-bladed knife on the stainless steel sink. The image horrified me as I visualised myself being cut open. Nobody told me what to expect, or what the procedure would be.

The screams of the other women got louder and louder as my contraction pains got sharper. And still nobody came to talk to me. The light was beginning to fade now, and though night was about to fall, I knew there would be no sleep. When the contractions got closer, I got off the table to visit the toilet, but I had no idea where it was. A nurse shouted at me to get back to my bed, but I insisted I needed to use the toilet. She showed me grudgingly to a cubicle.

The nurse came to visit me after what seemed a long time. Without as much as a word, she examined me and told me that she would be back shortly. The pain went beyond endurance. It was so bad that I considered using the knife on myself. I tried to breathe deeply as Emer had told me, but the pain broke through. All I could do was shout out. When the nurse did finally arrive, she told me to keep my voice down. I wasn't the only girl giving birth. This nurse had a sullen expression that never altered. I decided to be nice to her and to do everything she asked. She was about to deliver my baby, and I wanted her to look kindly on this new, precious life that was about to appear. She said nothing, not a word, as she prepared me for giving birth. The only time I remember hearing her voice was when she said, 'Don't push, until I tell you.'

My lovely baby girl was born at 11.40 am on July 18, 1967. The nurse placed her on my chest. Nothing else mattered now that she was here. I couldn't take my eyes away from her little face.

Again without a word, the nurse took my baby away and I looked up at her and said 'Thank you, Nurse, for delivering my baby safely.' There was no reply. Although the sullen expression never changed, somehow I knew my baby was in safe hands by the gentle way the nurse held my little girl. I thought, for an instant—or did I imagine it?—that I saw a half-smile flit across her face as she left the room.

Shortly afterwards, I was wheeled to the recovery section where there were other recovering mothers. My bed was at the end of a long row and I was glad to be at last able to sleep. I was woken up by a nurse who gave me a tablet. When I asked her what it was for, she said simply, 'It's to dry up your breast milk. Your baby won't be needing you.'

'Where is my baby? I want to see her. Is she alright?'

'Your baby is in the nursery with all the other babies, and she is being well cared for. You have done your work.'

We were allowed to visit the nursery twice a day when we changed nappies and bottle-fed our babies. My Bronagh was a beautiful, serene girl who rarely cried. It was Brian who had suggested the name Bronagh, both for the resonance of its rhythm and the shadow of sadness that it embodied; *brónach* is the word in Irish for 'sorrowful.' But I was deeply upset now. Where was Brian? I wanted him to know that we had a beautiful baby girl, and I wanted him to see her.

The highlight of our day was the two visits to the nursery to be with our babies. One morning, I noticed that a slight rash was appearing on Bronagh's little legs. When I pointed this out to the nurse, she immediately examined my hands. 'Do you wash your hands before handling your baby?' Of course I did! We were all meticulous about the importance of our rituals; we were like celebrants who washed their hands before going to the altar to perform the sacred act.

Our group of eight girls were all on the same timetabled schedule in the nursery. It was a happy place during our visiting hour, because the soft voices of the girls sung out in a chorus of ooohs and coos and nursery rhymes. After nappy-changing routine and washing our hands, we would sit in a circle bottle-feeding our babies. One girl would start singing and we would all join in. My song was always *Summer Time*, and a lump came into my throat when I sang, *So hush little baby, don't you cry...*

We were like a group of girls playing with our dolls, not having a care in the world. But not knowing what was ahead of us.

Brian did finally come to see me. The new dress that I had bought in St John's Wood fitted me perfectly. I ran towards him trying to make him believe that I was the same girl that he had fallen in love with. But the cruel pain between my legs told me that I wasn't.

'You look pale.' These were his first words. 'You poor pet!' We sat in the parlour talking stiffly; the smell of lavender polish and beeswax was smothering. He looked just the same. I wanted to ask him about the play he was directing, but the words dried up in my mouth.

I waited for him to ask to see the baby, but he didn't. The need in me for him to see the child we had both created overwhelmed me and I pulled him towards the nursery. Visitors were forbidden but the urge in me was so fierce that I pushed him towards the door against all the rules. I knew exactly where our baby was in the lines and lines of baby cots and made my way over to her. He took Bronagh up into his arms and kissed her. I was at peace now—at least for the next few weeks.

One day, about six weeks after the birth of Bronagh, Sister Joseph called me to the front parlour and said they had found a home for my baby. She would be going to a home in the midlands that afternoon when her new parents arrived.

When I told the girls they all congratulated me and said, 'You're free now. You have your life back again.' And I really believed them. Some of the girls had babies in the orphanage at the time, babies deemed unsuitable for adoption for many reasons, some because of the colour of their skin.

'You are one of the lucky ones. The nuns have found a good family for your baby.'

I spent the next few hours in a state of suspended shock. My baby would be going to a good home that would treasure her and provide everything that I couldn't. Wasn't that the right decision for any mother in my situation to make?

It was a sunny Sunday afternoon and a group of us were sitting on the flat part of the rooftop overlooking the front of the big house. 'A Whiter Shade of Pale' by Procol Harum, was playing on the transistor radio.

And so it was that later
As the miller told his tale
That her face, at first just ghostly
Turned a whiter shade of pale

And that was the moment I saw my Bronagh, wrapped in a white shawl, being carried out by her new mother who placed her in the waiting Moses basket in the back of a black car. My eyes followed the car until it disappeared out of sight.

Gone. All gone.

The girls stood up and applauded. It was our sincerely held belief that after our babies had been adopted we would walk out the gate of St Patrick's—born-again virgins—to start a new life.

'You're lucky she's going to a good place.'

'Yes,' I replied uncertainly.

'You can go home now. You're free.'

But I wasn't really free at all. Not in my mind, anyway. Little did I know then that a life sentence of sorts was about to begin.

My parents had thought I'd been living in Paris, that I had gone there after London. The nuns had a mother house in Rue du Bac in the 7th Arrondissement, where they sent all my letters. The French house would put my letters in an airmail envelope with a French postal code and redirect them to my parents. That was how they colluded with me in telling my story.

One of the nuns—I remember her lovely smiling face—said, 'Now Phyl, you will be returning to your parents' house from Paris. So we must fix you up with a nice French dress.' She brought me down to the needlework room and told me to choose from a selection of coloured fabrics. I chose a turquoise cloth.

One of the girls measured me and made my homecoming dress.

It is only now as I write this that I realise I didn't have to do any work with the nuns—I wasn't required to. Nor do I remember the girls ever talking about work. But that day I recall seeing girls sewing on machines when one of them measured me for my supposed Paris dress. I remember Emer working in the nursery, but it was something she volunteered for as her baby was still in one of those cots.

Brian drove me home to my parents' house that same day. Then he went back to his wife and children and to his theatrical life. My family didn't suspect a thing. They did ask, though, if I could now speak French.

It wasn't easy to pick up the threads of my life again. It wasn't like I had dropped a stitch of knitting and picked it up to continue the same pattern. I knew I had to find work, of course. But something was missing. A gaping hole that couldn't be filled.

I phoned the mother and baby home from a nearby phone box. I pressed button A. The money dropped into the belly of the coin box.

'I want my baby back, Sister.'

There was a long pause. I rambled on for a minute or two until the nun at the other end cut back in. 'If you don't stop whingeing, we'll have that baby on your mother's doorstep in the morning.'

The thought of my family finding out stopped me in my tracks. It would be an unspeakable disgrace. For evermore I would be a marked woman. Someone who had committed the biggest sin in Ireland at the time: having a child out of wedlock.

Miraculously, as it seemed to me at the time, a photograph arrived in the post with the image of my beautiful girl, smiling and happy. It had been sent by the Mother Superior. I remember wondering, at the time how, she had managed to get the photo to me so quickly. Surely she would have had to write to the new parents first? How did she know my correct name and address? It arrived a day or two after my phone call.

The picture put my mind at ease. My baby was in someone else's world now, and for better or for worse, I felt that she was at home there, loved and wanted. The letter was addressed to me under my real name—Phyl Herbert. It was a mystery to me how my real name emerged, because Brian had registered me under the name of Mary Hope.

When I finished gazing at the photo of the baby who had now grown bigger, had filled out and was smiling, I read the letter attached. It said simply that I had to attend a solicitor's office in Parnell Square. The words sent a chill through me. 'Please attend on Monday the 15th August at 3pm, to extinguish your parental rights to your birth baby. Your signature is required.'

To extinguish your parental rights....

But I did as I was told, at the appointed time.

It was becoming more and more difficult for me to continue living with my family. It was as though nothing had happened, because I couldn't speak about my trauma. Nor could I bear the awful, soul-crushing emptiness that each day brought. My family didn't know me now and I couldn't find a way to be open up to them.

Something had to be done and the distraction of a new job provided some relief, for a while.

Dublin in 1967 was supposedly a grey and dismal city. But that wasn't the way I saw it. My reality was different. The economic and social climate of the city didn't faze me at all, because my mind was set on other matters. Dublin to me was like an old overcoat I had become used to wearing because I didn't feel any need of a new one. What really mattered to me was where I lived, where I worked and who my friends were. When I say I didn't know my family any more, it might be more accurate to say my family didn't know me.

My younger sister, Eileen, was the only person to notice a change in me. One day, when we had the house to ourselves she said, 'You don't laugh anymore.'

I was on the verge of opening up to her.

'What did those Frogs do to you, Phyl?' Then I couldn't stop laughing.

My friend Claire had emigrated to England by this time. She was the only other person who knew my story, apart from Brian and his wife.

I was fortunate in finding the Joan Morrison Employment Agency in Dame Street, who sent me for an interview with Allen Figgis, publisher and managing director of Hodges Figgis bookshop in Dawson Street. They had a position for a personal assistant. Once again, my typing skills were my passport to the job.

'Start on Monday. You are a brilliant typist.' At least there was one thing in life I was good at, I thought to myself. After a few weeks working in Hodges Figgis one of the girls told me about a flat that was vacant in Baggot Street. I didn't need to be told a second time.

Working for Allen was like being in a completely new world. I met a lot of different people during those first weeks. People like Brendan Kennelly and Derek Mahon, writers who called in to see Allen. The girls on the shop floor were friendly to me. I got on particularly well with one, Anne, who worked in the paperback section. When we went for lunch every day, she would fill me in on all the people that she met that morning. One day she told me that an actor from the Focus Theatre had come into the shop asking her to put up a poster. The words at the end of the poster were the words that caught my attention:

All enquiries about our Acting Studio, phone 736071

ON STAGE

11. THE FOCUS

It was a sunny Saturday afternoon in October 1967 when I turned into Pembroke Lane. The year of Vietnam, the Summer of Love, the Six-Day War, Sergeant Pepper...

The laneway was flanked by a row of 19th-century cottages. Opposite these stood a nondescript building with a flat roof. The long white-painted brick wall was featureless except for a black door at one end. It was slightly open. Surely a sign that I could walk in without knocking. Low voices tinkled through the darkness. I stood still for a moment to get my bearings.

A halo emerged through the shaft of light, framing a woman with a head of reddish, blonde hair. For a moment I thought I was seeing an apparition. It was Deirdre O'Connell, the legendary founder and director of the Focus Theatre. She was dressed entirely in black and standing on the stage with her arms outstretched, as if invoking the gods. Then I spotted a man on a ladder adjusting a stage lamp. 'Hold that there, Deirdre.'

Deirdre stepped off the stage to place the bulb on a seat and spotted me. Her face lit up in a smile. 'You must be Phyl...come and sit over here.' She looked up at the man on the ladder.

'We have a visitor, Tom.'

It was then that I realised I knew this man from television. It was 'Benjy'! The actor Tom Hickey! I watched him every Sunday evening in *The Riordans*, one of Ireland's first rural drama series. His name was a byword in every household, and the gormless, country-cute character he played was one of the pivots of *The Riordans*.

'That's it,' he said. 'All sorted.'

My eyes fixed on his brown suede shoes as he climbed down the ladder. He wasn't dressed a bit like Benjy from the television. No mucky turned-down wellies. The suede jacket was a tasteful match for the shoes too. He walked towards me, to the edge of the stage. Then he sat down with his feet dangling right in front of where I was sitting, the toes of his suede shoes almost touching mine. Without a word, he leaned his head towards me as if he was looking for something in my face. He didn't speak for what seemed like a long time.

Then he leaned backwards and said, almost as an afterthought, 'I saw your photo in Arnott's.'

What did he mean? Me, in Arnott's, the large department store in Henry Street?

He thought a moment. 'You're the image of one of those beautiful women hanging on the wall up there, in their new gallery.' Was he trying to make fun of me? I couldn't really tell. I didn't know what to say, so I said nothing at all.

Deirdre saw I was confused and embarrassed and tried to put me at my ease. 'I think he likes you,' she said with a little smile.

When Tom Hickey left the studio, Deirdre took out her folder and wrote down my name and details. The weekly rates for being a member of the Focus Studio were so low that I wondered how she could possibly survive on such little money. The salary from my new job in the bookshop left me with ample spare cash for the fee, even after paying the rent. I watched the pen move slowly across the page as she wrote my name into her folder. I was captivated by her clear, musical voice, peppered with traces of her New York origins. She explained how the studio classes worked and told me that I could sit in and observe her class that day. I couldn't stop staring at her eyelashes. They were the longest I'd ever seen. And there wasn't a trace of make-up on her pale face. Her blue eyes actually sparkled. I had never met anybody like her before.

'After the class you can decide if you want to join us here next weekend.'

Deirdre then went up the few steps to the back of the theatre with her clipboard under her arm.

'Beautiful.' Had Tom really described me as beautiful? Had I heard correctly? Was I really like one of those beautiful women of 1967 in Arnott's? I would have to visit the shop and see that exhibition. But would he think I was still beautiful if he knew the secret I was hiding? Would anyone?

Brian had never told me I was beautiful, though he did once say 'You have nice eyes.' When I said I didn't, he said simply, 'Well, to me you have.' And took the good out of his half-hearted compliment.

Later that day I sat alone in the front row sensing that something serious was about to happen. I took in everything in the little theatre while I waited for the class to begin. The seats were covered in autumnal shades of gold and mustard, toning in with the burnt orange of the heavy stage curtains. Everything seemed just right. I counted the ten seats on my row and then looked behind me to count the nine rows slanting upwards towards the entrance. Before I had finished counting, the door into the auditorium opened and a group of striking-looking young women entered, one more beautiful than the next. There was a lot of excited chat with Deirdre, then a few more people arrived and spread themselves out in the rows behind me.

At 2pm the class began. The theatre fell silent. It was like being at a film, but this was real. The actors were all within touching distance of each other on the stage. I could almost feel their breath on my skin. It was far better than the cinema because this was the very essence of theatre. Every performance was unique and unrepeatable. Everybody present would be showing their work to Deirdre, who was calling out the order of events.

The first activity was the mirror exercise. Deirdre's final command was 'House lights down.' Mary Elizabeth Burke-Kennedy arrived on stage. A young man joined her. The first thing I noticed when she was under the lights was the vibrant colour of Mary Elizabeth's trouser suit—emerald green. It was my first time to see a woman wearing such an outfit. She looked so feminine and beautiful, and I wanted to find out where I could buy an outfit just like that. What was wrong with me, I wondered?

How come I hadn't taken in all the changes that were happening all around me? I didn't have to remind myself, of course, that for almost the past year I had been out of circulation. Or to put it another way, I had been in hiding, not thinking about the latest fashions in clothes. I did know, though, that women were forbidden to wear trousers in their place of work. Until recently, women students hadn't been allowed wear trousers when entering the library in UCD.

It was magic watching Mary Elizabeth's liquid body movements as she moved across the stage, with the young man doing his best to follow her. Would I have the confidence to let myself go like that?

I observed two more young women on the Focus stage that afternoon. One woman had acted in *Play with a Tiger* by Doris Lessing. She was exploring the character of an old woman for her next role. I could not believe the transformation that took place in a matter of moments. With the subtlest of movements, the girl became an old woman. When she spoke, her voice had completely altered. It was as if she had been possessed by the ghost of the old character she was about to play in Chekhov's *Uncle Vanya*. That young woman was Sabina Coyne, now Sabina Higgins, wife of the man who would be President of Ireland, Michael D Higgins.

This alchemy was what Deirdre facilitated through her Stanislavski teachings. There were no gimmicks and no masks. All the transformative changes were brought about by deep psychological analysis of the roles being explored.

Joan Bergin was on the other side of the stage at the same time that Sabina was performing her exercise. She was like a film star. Her hair was the same colour as Deirdre's, yet different. A long plait hung elegantly over one shoulder. A long, multicoloured skirt swished as she moved around the stage. Long skirts, another new fashion that I wasn't aware of! This exercise was 'Justification of an Object'. Joan's voice began to change as she opened a little jewellery box.

With each piece of jewellery, her body movements quickened until it seemed that she was almost dancing. I watched these two women engage with utter intensity as they explored the worlds of their chosen characters. It was alchemy at work, and I was hypnotised.

Later on, I learned more about these three women. Joan worked for Irish Ropes and travelled to faraway places like Norway, Sweden and Germany—countries that I had only seen in my school geography books. Countries where she bought her glamorous clothes. Sabina worked in the civil service, and Mary Elizabeth was a teacher in Muckross Park College, a girls' secondary school in the well-off suburb of Donnybrook.

At the end of the class the three women sat on the edge of the stage, where Tom Hickey had been sitting only a few hours earlier, and listened to Deirdre's feedback. 'What is your objective? What were you trying to achieve?' Deirdre asked each of them in turn.

These two questions resonated with me, and with my own life. I sensed new energy infusing my bloodstream, seeping into that aching void that had appeared only weeks earlier.

'My objective was to show how my character expressed her struggle with her ageing body and her great need to be heard in the household,' Sabina said.

Deirdre's voice dropped a notch. 'You mean, Sabina, that she wasn't accepting her diminishing role in family matters.' Deirdre went on to say that Sabina had achieved what she had set out to do. That the physical characterisation of the grandmother had been excellent.

These people were so articulate, and I wanted to be just like them. I now had a new path in life to explore, I told myself. Three weekends later I took part in a series of introductory group exercises and became friendly with other new members.

Treasa lived near me, and after class we would walk home together. Her flat was in Herbert Place, a few minutes' walk from mine in Baggot Street. I didn't tell Treasa about Bronagh, even though it might have been easier to share my secret with a stranger, because I was trying to forge a new identity for myself—and trying to forget. We were also so consumed by the studio classes and plays being performed in the evenings that we rarely spoke about our private lives.

The first job beginners were given was to help out during the coffee break. The coffee room was at the back of the stage. Tucked away in the corner was the toilet. Our job was to collect the milk from the family who lived in the houses opposite. The Tobin family were central to the running of the theatre. They were the neighbours who kept an eye on the place.

Deirdre insisted on a high standard of cleanliness, and paid particular attention to how this little coffee room was presented. Fresh flowers in tiny vases adorned the coffee ledges around the room. The walls were festooned with photographs of the productions. One showed Mary Elizabeth dancing with abandon during her role as a gypsy in Strindberg's *Miss Julie*. The photo beside it featured Deirdre as Miss Julie herself. Chekhov's play *The Wedding*, with Mary Elizabeth playing the bride, was on a double bill with *Miss Julie*. During the run of these plays, Mary Elizabeth's father died, and I took over both her roles.

It was 1968 now, the year of my first acting role in the Focus Theatre. In later years, every time I looked at those photos, I looked for myself among the images, but, of course, I wasn't there. I had only acted as a stand-in for Mary Elizabeth. On a separate wall, all to itself, was a luminous portrait by Fergus Bourke of the enigmatic Deirdre. She deserved a whole wall to herself.

Some evenings Treasa and I would visit Margaret Gaj's restaurant on Baggot Street and treat ourselves to her famous French toast with bacon and pineapple. One night as we were leaving Gaj's, Luke Kelly and Ronnie Drew from The Dubliners arrived with a group of people and Treasa nodded over at Luke's mass of curly red hair. 'Did you know Deirdre is married to Luke?' I couldn't believe it. Deirdre in the role of wife was unthinkable to me.

My turn to explore an exercise eventually came. Over several weekends I had been involved in group work such as movement, vocal exercises and improvisation. Deirdre said, 'I have an animal study for you, Phyl. An animal of your choice.' The task was to visit the zoo and study an animal, to observe its movements, its way of being, its very essence. The next stage was to integrate and translate elements of the animal into a human personality—a personality with a story.

I had been to Dublin Zoo a couple of times, once on my confirmation day and another time when I brought my little niece, Katherine. My favourites were the penguins, lions, tigers and cheetahs. I would wait until I made my visit before deciding on which animal to analyse. The number 10 bus to the Phoenix Park and the zoo stopped right outside my flat. Early one Saturday morning, I set off on my mission and walked around the zoological gardens. The monkey house, the giraffes and the elephants were all enjoyable to observe, but nothing about them spoke to me. What did I have in common with any of them, anyway?

And then I saw her, in all her grandeur: a great white polar bear. She seemed to be bidding me to come and look at her. She had appeared from nowhere and was standing on her hind legs as if to say, 'Look at me! Look at my stomach,' as she patted that area in a circular motion. Was she showing me that she was pregnant? It was almost as if she had emerged from the stone. Her eyes bored right into mine; I felt an immediate connection with the beautiful beast. I had found my spirit animal, a pregnant soul all alone on the edge of a cold and deserted corner, deep in a pit of emptiness. I wanted to possess this beautiful bear and take her home with me. But all I could do was lean on the fence and study her huge white bulk.

I watched her land on all fours and saunter away in a slow meditative pace along the rocky ledge. I imagined her thoughts. *You know me now. Go home now and make me your own character.* I walked on towards the exit, carrying the spirit of this mamma white polar bear in my heart.

I don't remember being heavy when I was carrying Bronagh, though I do recall how swollen my body was. My baby had never been such a heavy burden. It was more my image of being enlarged that weighed me down. And the fact that I was carrying my secret on my body, for all the world to see. No such guilt existed in the animal world. I would explore that fact as one of my objectives when my turn came in the studio class.

I had to find a real character to embody in my exercise. My character, I decided, should be a beautiful woman with an adoring husband. My preparations for this study had now begun. I walked back towards the bus, silently exploring the idea of being a happy woman, proceeding cautiously because of the weight I was carrying. Watching where I placed my foot, one careful step at a time. Lovingly stroking my stomach with its precious new life inside. Grateful that I was starting a family and about to become a perfect mother.

I could hear Deirdre's voice inside my head saying, 'Feel the emotion, Phyl. Let your body express it. Let your voice carry it.' I walked towards the bus stop chanting these words in my head.

This pregnant woman possessed my every waking moment during the week. Though my job in Hodges Figgis kept me busy enough, sometimes Allen would say, half-joking, 'When are you going to give up that play-acting, Phyl?' By the time my next class arrived, I had filled in the background of this woman. I knew what her objectives were during her pregnancy.

The three golden elements in a Stanislavski study are The Objective of the Exercise, The Circumstances of the World of the Character, and The Activity (allowing the movement to progress the storyline). These were not only valuable techniques for me to absorb for my future development as a director, but also the scaffolding for me to build my later fiction.

Saturday came and it was my turn to take the stage. 'Right, Phyl, let's see how your animal study is progressing.'

My activity was to pack my suitcase for the hospital and select the items I wanted to take with me. At this stage, we were all well-versed in what our objectives were or should be. I wanted to tell my husband how much I loved him—and what to do if I did not survive the birth of our baby. The set-up for this improvisation was that the actor playing my husband was to enter the stage with a surprise gift. The improvisation would develop from that point. I took up my space on the stage and walked around, stroking my stomach like the big polar bear. Then I looked out into the darkness of the theatre. For a moment, I was back in St Patrick's Mother and Baby Home, not knowing what to do next. Not knowing what was going to happen to my baby.

Still waiting for Brian to rescue me...

John, my actor husband, entered the stage carrying a big carton on wheels. 'Look what I have for my beautiful wife.' He came towards me and kissed my cheek. 'You're looking a bit flushed darling.' I could feel my temperature rising. He sat me down. 'Close your eyes.'

I waited until he had uncovered the contents. 'Our baby's new white cot!' It was then that I started to cry in earnest. Little sobs came first and then big gulping sighs that rose up from my very depths. All I could see were the white cots from Bronagh's nursery and the empty cot that lay bare in front of me. I could hear Deirdre's sigh of approval in the back seat of the theatre.

I slipped back slowly into my role on the stage. After the exercise was completed Deirdre, said, 'Phyl, you did it...got right inside your character. Your emotional display of joy was superb!' I knew now that somewhere deep down, I had a well of emotional history to draw from. And it wasn't one of joy, as Deirdre thought.

The theatre wasn't the only thing to take up my energies. University was beckoning to me, and the education I had missed out on. And, if theatre was the force that salved my broken heart and helped to somehow fill the gap in my life, study would help order my thinking and pull me back out of myself again.

12. UCD

University College Dublin, on Earlsfort Terrace, just off St Stephen's Green. It was my first time inside a university building. All I could see were hundreds of people, men and women of all ages, hustling for a place in the queue. I spotted Ruth, whom I knew to see. She was smiling over at me, the only familiar face on the BA queue, so I joined her.

'I know you from Hayes, Conyngham and Robinson's'—the big chemist shop on Grafton Street.'

'And you're the new girl with Allen Figgis.'

Ruth had a self-possessed air about her—a girl who was always definite about things. Her sallow complexion and blonde hair made her stand out in the queue. Her dress was meticulous, a crispy white blouse peeping from under the collar of her navy blue gabardine coat. She was a real beauty.

'What subjects are you enrolling in?' I asked her.

'English. I want to learn more about poetry.'

'English is my first subject choice too. But don't we have to choose another three?' I chose philosophy, archaeology, and French.

After evening lectures, Ruth and I would walk home together, each to our own bedsit, two young women in our early twenties, both on a merry go-round of discovering university life. Leaving my parents' house had been like moving to another country and meeting people who spoke a different language. This was a new step. Every move away from my old life was a new opportunity to forget.

New foundations were slowly emerging. The compass points of my new world were all within walking distance. The Focus Theatre was around the corner off Pembroke Street, a ten-minute walk from my flat on Baggot Street and my new job was just down the road on Dawson Street. The territory around the university on Earlsfort Terrace would be the little patch of the city where I took my first steps towards becoming a new me.

One evening after a meeting of the English Lit Society I said to Ruth, 'You never told me you wrote poetry?'

Ruth was a very private person and never revealed much about herself. She shrank back a little. 'I can't believe you chose both of my poems to read.' It had been our first time at a meeting of the writers' group organised by the English Lit. We sat around a table, on which the student chairing the meeting had emptied a bag full of submitted work, each folded so as not to reveal the name of the author. We had to select two items and then take turns to read them aloud. After I read out the two I had chosen, there was silence for a while, followed by a long discussion on the nature of the poems. One person compared Ruth's writing to Beckett. Her identity was now out within the group. Both poems were later published in *St Stephen's*, the university magazine.

Ruth and I both firmly believed that we could change the world. The older generation didn't understand that we could now think for ourselves. We didn't listen to what was being said from the pulpit anymore, because we had stopped attending mass. There was a real sense of impending change in the late 1960s in Dublin and an undercurrent of rebellion in the air. Marches against America's involvement in the Vietnam War took pace all across Europe. Young people were questioning the old mores that had been handed down. In Ireland, students were also revolting against the universities' governing bodies who decided the rules and courses, excluding students from decision-making.

I don't know if anything changed very much in UCD as a result of the so-called 'Gentle Revolution'. But being a student at the philosophy lectures of Denys Turner changed my life. It all came together one particular night when he introduced a new topic, the existentialism of Jean Paul Sartre. This was for me the Holy Grail from the mouth of this softly spoken Englishman. His words represented a sort of cleansing, a new baptism. I felt renewed. I was starting to see life—and my own life, in particular—from a different perspective.

'It doesn't matter what the circumstances of your birth are, what mistakes you've made in your past, you and you alone are the sole creator of your own destiny, your own scriptwriter. It is up to each one of us to decide what we want in life.' I can still hear Denys Turner's distinctive English accent.

The words went straight to the centre of my confused identity as he glided from one side of the podium to the other, his hands pushing the curly hair back from his young face. His words were dynamite to me because I now felt absolved of all my so-called sins. His words hinted too at a bigger world out there, waiting for me. Only one other person in my world had spoken like this before, and that was Deirdre O'Connell. It was a reiteration of Deirdre's core teachings: find your character and build from there.

It was the last night of our first term in UCD. I was looking for Ruth in the Annexe, the student canteen in the basement of Earlsfort Terrace. It was a cold night and the queue for hot food was longer than usual. Beans, egg and chips were filling up all the waiting trays. There was no sign of Ruth. As I looked around, I thought that I spotted Brian talking to a group of women at a nearby table. No, no, it couldn't be, could it? It had been ages since we'd last seen each other. In fact, not since the night he left me home from St Patrick's. Then I heard Ruth call me. I headed over to her and put Brian out of my mind.

During the final English lecture, I listened intently to Jim O'Malley, lecturer in Drama, talking about Pirandello: something about the playwright seeing a man coming towards him, but when the man comes into focus he is wearing rouge and lipstick. O'Malley was talking about the concept of 'mask' in modern drama, how Pirandello was one of the few playwrights to delve into the complex nature of the human psyche. O'Malley spoke about the many faces people have, and the playwright's theme, always the complexity of the human condition.

Jim himself was involved in Dramsoc, the UCD dramatic society, and I later acted in his production of Ben Jonson's *Bartholomew Fair*. He liked to throw out questions and statements to the lecture hall. This night he asked, 'Do we ever know a person fully?'

The question was rattling around in my head, sparking all sorts of speculation, when I saw her in the middle distance. She was chewing the end of her biro and looking around the lecture hall. She didn't see me, but I kept my eyes fixed firmly on her. How could I not have noticed her before now? Weeks before, she had buttonholed me in Hodges Figgis—through clever detective work—and warned me to stay away from her husband.

'Would you like to come out for a coffee?' were her opening words that day. I looked at her blankly. Who was this unknown woman? Had she mistaken me for someone else, or had I simply forgotten her face? In the Irish History section of the bookshop, she backed me into a corner before saying, 'I think we have a friend in common.' She was quite civilised about it all, but her instructions were quite clear. 'If you ever contact my husband again, I will tell your parents everything. And I mean *everything*.'

This encounter with Brian's wife brought back all of the pain I thought I had buried. Not even Sartre or Denys Turner's soft voice could help me now.

I waited until she had left the lecture hall to make my way out of the university, down the front steps of Earlsfort Terrace. A group of us had arranged to meet in Hartigan's pub on Leeson Street for a final Christmas drink. On my way across the road, I spotted them, hand in hand, chuckling. When his eyes met mine, the chuckling stopped. He threw me a wink as much as to say 'I'm back with her now.'

No, you never really know anybody. That much was sadly true. But I still couldn't believe how casual his behaviour had been. And how the sight of him still stirred something in me, despite myself.

13. THE SHAKES

I met Eilis Mullan in the English Literature class in 1970, the year UCD moved out to Belfield on the southern outskirts of the city. At the end of lectures, students usually met up in the new bar on the campus. It was a big change from the pubs in Leeson Street. There were no nooks and crannies to hide in, no golden, smoke-stained ceilings. After a few pints our voices would rise. Eilis's voice was always the loudest. Myself, Celia and Paul, my new friends in Belfield, would watch her exhale and, as the smoke curlicued towards the ceiling, we would wait for her review of the evening's lecture. 'It's a pity they don't know how to project.' And then, after another sip of her Smithwicks, she would add, 'They really should be trained in the art of acting. After all, aren't we their captive audience?'

Eilis was a little older than the rest of us, but her long strawberry blonde hair and slim figure were altogether ageless. Nobody dared to tie her down to any particular year of birth. Younger men adored her. She had that big sister status. Nobody dared interrupt her. When she started to talk her voice was like a train chugging out of a station and we knew to wait until she came to a halt. Only then did we dare offer a comment.

When she spoke about her involvement in the Dublin Shakespeare Society I listened particularly carefully.

'What do you actually do there, Eilis?' She took a long drag on her cigarette and held my gaze before exhaling her answer. 'Everything.'

'Including acting?' I thought she'd make a good actress.

'Oh, God, no! I leave that to the members of the studio.'

Eilis was the chairperson of the committee and the organiser of the annual programme—the main event being whatever Shakespeare play was on the Leaving Certificate. She was also the stage manager and the person who really held the reins.

A few weeks later, she asked me about my time in the Focus. 'I hear they train actors there.'

'Yes. The Stanislavski method.'

'I thought the only way to train actors was to give them a script and let them work their way through it? Isn't it all down to stage miles, when all is said and done?' She angled her head and fixed me in her gaze.

'Well, no. The training off-script is what it's all about.'

I was holding everyone's attention, for once. Eilis wasn't that interested in the theory of acting. She didn't speak for a long time then took a long drag on her cigarette, exhaled the smoke slowly and said, 'Improvisation, you mean? No script? Actors will never buy that.'

'Nowhere to hide,' I said.

She considered this for a moment. Then she spoke again. 'Would you be interested in giving a workshop in the Shakes?'

This invitation to the Dublin Shakespeare Society from Eilis turned out to be a life-changing moment for me.

An Actor Prepares is the Bible according to Stanislavski. I had not only studied it but lived its pages. Now it was my time to prepare. As Deirdre used to say, 'The minute you make an entrance, you should displace air.' I was ready for this role, or I was about to be ready, anyway. There was little for me to prepare by way of workshop content. However, I really did want to work on a new image for myself.

My flatmate, Sandra, had made me a denim midi-skirt. My brown cowboy boots, showing just enough leather at the end of the scalloped hemline, would be a perfect match. I must look like someone who knew what they were about. My almost-new musquash fur jacket from Stock Xchange, the second-hand clothes shop on Baggot Street, was my pride and joy. It was my mantle of sophistication. My crowning glory was my Afro hairstyle. For once in my life my curly hair was in fashion. I didn't have to fight nature anymore.

It was a crisp October evening when I walked up North Great George's Street, past the grand line of Georgian houses. I passed what had been the Unicorn Theatre on the left of the road. The theatre people had been smoked out like an unwelcome swarm of bees by economic realities. What a different girl I was now, I thought, from that gullible young woman who had allowed herself to be seduced by a married man. If he could see me now, what would he think?

And should I really care what he thought? There were rumours that he had been seen hand-in-hand with a young actress from one of his Damer productions, no doubt someone who could flirt with him *as Gaeilge*. What did I care? I was stepping out on a new path. He was past tense now and I was busy forging myself into a new woman.

I descended the basement steps at the Shakes. My boots squeaked as I landed on the path leading to the open door. It was a little bit like the Unicorn, I had to admit, but I brushed the image away. My eyes seized on a flash of shiny colours and I knew immediately I was in new territory: a stained-glass image of Shakespeare covered the entire back wall of the entrance—liberated from the old Capitol Cinema off O'Connell Street, Eilis told me. (That same stained-glass image of Shakespeare is now housed in the Teachers' Club on Parnell Square.)

'Is that you, Phyl?' I heard Eilis's voice coming from inside. The space was much the same as the Focus and the Unicorn, raked seating and a raised stage, with heavy black curtains at either side.

'Let me light this Super Ser before we do anything.' She turned on the gas heater and offered me a cigarette, and we both lit up.

'You're early. Follow me and I'll show you what's out here before they arrive.'

It was dark as we walked down the passageway and into the dressing room.

Eilis turned on a switch. 'Jesus, Mary and Holy Saint Joseph! What's going on here?'

There were coats and trousers strewn on the floor. 'Men! How can anyone live with them?'

She reached for the empty clothes hangers and placed the garments neatly on the rail. 'They must have been in a hurry before closing time.'

'What was the play?'

'The Shadow of a Gunman, part of our studio programme. We hire out bigger theatres for the Shakespearian plays for schools.'

I learned that a Shakespeare play was produced each year and students from schools all over Ireland would attend. My friends Celia and Paul were involved in these. Celia was the costume designer and Paul was not only the sound engineer but also selected the music for every production.

Eilis shrugged her shoulders. 'Let's get back to the heat, Phyl.' But it wasn't warm enough for me to take off my musquash coat just yet.

'The loo is out in the back, but you'd have to be in a bad way to use it.' She pointed in the direction of an open area like a yard. Beyond that I could just about make out the shape of a door. 'It's open to the elements and there's no roof. Better to wait until we get to Tony Bourke's pub later.'

We returned to the auditorium and the stuttering glow of gas flames from the Super Ser. A chill ran down my back with the cold now. I stood up and started to stretch my arms in a circle to warm myself. A group of young men arrived in and looked in my direction, grinning. 'You must be the woman from that crazy place,' one of them said.

'Shusssh!' Eilis hissed and put her index finger to her mouth as if she were talking to schoolchildren.

I knew he meant the Focus, but I ignored the question. Two more young women arrived and that made five people for the workshop. Eilis gave a brief introduction and sat on a side seat near the door. I talked first about the importance of being physically at ease on stage. I felt confident because I knew what

I was about to facilitate. My plan for the evening was to introduce the Mirror Exercise and then a simple improvisation.

Eventually we got started, and after going through a brief process of relaxation and breathing I began to set the session in motion. 'I'd like you to stand opposite each other.' There was one person who didn't have a partner, so I got up on the stage and stood facing him. 'Decide who will lead and then just follow their movements'

I began to move my arms and looked around at the other pairs. They hadn't moved an inch. They were looking in Eilis's direction as if seeking to be rescued from this torture chamber.

'Imagine you are seeing your reflection in the mirror. Follow the movement.' The only person who wasn't giggling now was my partner, Harry. He made it easy for me because he got the instruction immediately. His concentration was intense, but I could see that he was flexible and quite unselfconscious. We moved on to mime activities and eventually the group relaxed and began to concentrate. 'Forget about dialogue. Focus on activity and clarity of movement.'

I gave the group a simple exercise in improvisation where they devised a situation which involved dialogue in a work setting. The ice was broken now, and I was beginning to feel myself possessed by the spirit of Deirdre and the Focus.

Afterwards, we strolled around the corner to the snug in Tony Bourke's pub on Hill Street. After ordering our pints, there was a tidal rush by the young men to sit beside Eilis. Nobody mentioned the workshop. It was as if nothing had happened. As if I hadn't been there. I didn't know what to make of it. When closing time was called, Harry asked me if he could buy me another pint.

While he was at the bar, I overheard one of the giggling boys say to Eilis, 'I went to see that Russian Hamlet last Saturday, in the Astor cinema. God, I'd love to learn how to act like that.'

Harry returned with our drinks, 'Here's to you, Phyl. And thank you for a great workshop.'

I wasn't expecting to be invited back, but I was wrong. The workshop sessions proved very effective and they formed a part of the studio programme over the next few months. Harry was still the most enthusiastic member. He had a serious interest in developing his acting skills. One night in Tony Bourke's, he turned to me.

'I'd love to be in a play directed by you, Phyl.' Then he looked over at Eilis. She was a little taken aback. 'Oh, Harry, you know the rules. I'd have to put that to the committee.'

And so it came to pass. It would be my first time to direct a play—and one of my own choosing, too. This was a huge opportunity for me and one that I knew would never have arisen in the Focus Theatre.

Dublin was a city waiting to explode. If the 1960s was the decade when the outside world finally penetrated into our culture, the 1970s was the decade when the dams of silence finally burst. I had recently been to see Edward Albee's play *Who's Afraid of Virginia Woolf* at the Olympia Theatre. It had marked a turning point in my experience of plays on an Irish stage. Never before had I seen a married couple shout and scream obscenities at each other on the stage. I loved—quite literally—the drama of it all. The play was performed by a visiting English company as part of the Dublin Theatre Festival. While I'd certainly seen superb acting at the Focus, this play contained superb writing, and the storyline pushed the boundaries of whatever I had seen before. I had never heard of Edward Albee, but I knew that I wanted to learn more about him.

Accordingly, the play I chose was *The American Dream*—a play with a cast of just five. I was fortunate to discover Deborah Coulter, an American woman who had joined my workshop. She had no inhibitions about exploring emotional situations in our improvisations. Harry was the obvious choice for the young man in the play. The one problem of casting was who would play the grandmother. When I was sitting in Tony Bourke's one night with Eilis, I had a moment of enlightenment. Sitting right in front of me, drinking her pint and smoking her cigarette, was the very woman I wanted to play the part: Eilis herself. It took a lot of persuasive energy, but eventually she relented. Rehearsals for *The American Dream* began. It was 1973 and the posters were printed for a December run.

Harry and Deborah led the way during rehearsals when I introduced improvisations off-text. This practice was used in the Focus to build the credibility of character relationships. Little by little, there was a loosening out, and at times it seemed like a real ensemble was emerging. Harry played the young rebel with gusto, perhaps too much gusto at times.

He would often visit me in my new flat in Pembroke Road for a private run-through of his lines before rehearsals. His pretext was that he wanted to explore his vocal range. I engaged with him fully. I loved his enthusiasm and his eagerness to explore any improvisational situation I presented. After all, a good performance from Harry would reflect well on his director. One evening I set up the scenario of a lover's quarrel, where I took on the role of his partner. Sparks flew, like in the Edward Albee play. These improvisations became very real and, at the time, I was too involved in the character to pay any attention to Harry's emotions. 'Wonderful,' I would say every time he reached a vocal climax. The more I praised him the more expressive he became

The play was a huge success. Members old and new flocked to the studio to see Eilis's debut stage performance. At times, the applause was so out of kilter with the dramatic situation that Eilis found it difficult to stay in character and had to turn her back to the audience in order to recover her composure. Even though it was my debut as a director, and the committee members didn't really approve of the change, they grudgingly acknowledged that I had achieved a new high in production levels for the Shakes.

At the closing night party Harry tried to direct me towards a nearby bedroom. 'I think I'm falling in love with you, Phyl.' He took my hands in his and said, 'I've never met anyone like you. Can I see you again?' It felt like he was talking to someone else. The words just seemed like words from some dry script. And how could he possibly find me attractive, I thought. I'm damaged goods. At another level, I was quietly flattered, while reminding myself that Harry was a married man. I couldn't go through another relationship that had to be hidden from the world I knew that territory all too well. Or believed that I did.

One Saturday afternoon I found myself minding a stall in the Dandelion Market on St Stephen's Green. Celia, who had to give up her job in the civil service as a result of the marriage bar (women civil servants then had to give up their jobs if they got married), had set up a stall. She was a creative person. As well as being a costume designer for the theatre, she could crochet and design shawls and other fine garments. The market was the centre of action in the city at the weekends. Occasionally, I would relieve her for an hour or so while she took her lunch break.

I watched Celia as she walked under the archway with her husband, Jack Harte, and I thought, how lovely to have a partner that you can share all your creative life with. Jack was about to start a literary and music session in the Pembroke Pub on Pembroke Street with writers and musicians. He had recently started his new Profile Press imprint, and some of his books were on the stall.

Sitting at the stall was like being in the audience of a new outdoor drama. I loved watching the cast of characters as they passed. Women were wearing miniskirts or midis. Men were letting their hair grow longer and weren't afraid to wear the odd earring. Sometimes it really was hard to tell the difference between men and women.

There was something about one woman as she approached the entrance to the market that caught my eye. It was the way she was talking animatedly to the man she was with. His hand was on her shoulder. They walked by the stall, with only eyes for each other. I thought to myself: that is exactly what I want in a relationship. Then I looked more closely at the man. It was Brian. My Brian, with someone else. So the rumours were true then! I had heard that he had left his wife and children and was living with a younger woman. Younger than me too, as it happened. She was an actress who had been in his play at the Damer—obviously the person I had heard about: the one who could make love *as Gaeilge*. Did he ever think of me now, or of our lovely daughter? Did his new girlfriend even know about us? How could he forget so quickly?

The world seemed suddenly flat and featureless to me. Why didn't he look at me? I wanted to be that woman with his hand on my shoulder. I was right back there again, feeling that I was missing something, a lost part of myself. I quickly picked up a book from the stall to distract myself and vowed that I would put this episode out of my mind.

After my BA, I did the Higher Diploma in Education to qualify as a teacher, which meant another year travelling out to lectures in Belfield. It also meant that I would have to find teaching hours in a second-level school, which I managed to do in Clogher Road Vocational School in Kimmage, where many young student teachers gained their HDip hours.

During my time in the school I formed new friendships with three special people: Carmel O'Rourke, Gabriel Byrne and Sheila Murray. The staff room was a buzzing place where all the teachers appeared at different times of the day. It was over an afternoon coffee break that a conversation with Gabriel Byrne revealed that he too was interested in theatre. At this time he was a regular film-goer, and he often wrote reviews for film magazines. He told me he would like to act in a play. I told him about my involvement with the Dublin Shakespeare Society.

One of the Shakes' actors, Daniel Stokes, a teacher from St Patrick's secondary school near Christ Church, had written an abridged version of *Coriolanus* for his students. He told me that he was impressed by my production of *The American Dream* and asked me if I would be interested in directing his play. This was an opportunity for me to explore Shakespearian drama on a small scale, so I said that I would.

I told Gabriel about this new venture, inviting him to the auditions. I cast him as Aufidius, his first acting role. Gabriel was in his early twenties then. To describe him as dark and handsome would be an actionable understatement. He had the most disarming smile, and a wicked sense of humour to match his quick wit and incisive intelligence. I cast Daniel Stokes as Coriolanus. Daniel was tall and blond, a foil for Gabriel's dark looks. During rehearsals, a cast member left with short notice before opening night, so I took over his part as one of the citizens at the last minute. All the cast were dressed in black for the production. It was a marvellous dramatic statement—or so we thought then—and we felt we were really breaking into new theatrical territory with this production.

One Saturday, after rehearsals, Gabriel and I were walking along Parnell Street. Passing the Gate Theatre, he looked over and pointed at the building, 'One day, Phyl, I expect to see your name up there.' We both laughed at that.

As it turned out of, course, it was not my name that would go up in lights, but his. And that was never a surprise. I had sensed for some time that his destiny lay beyond our little drama group, somewhere beyond our reach.

The workshop production of *Coriolanus* was a huge success. Carmel and Sheila from Clogher Road attended one night. When we were having a drink later in the Belvedere Hotel opposite the theatre, Carmel confided that she thought Gabriel was smitten with me. This came as a huge surprise, and of course I was flattered. I did my best to ignore his tender attentions. It wasn't only the fact that I was a few years older than him, but I still thought myself unworthy of engaging in any romantic relationships. It would have been totally out of the question to reveal to him that I was a woman with a past. Someone who had dallied with a married man and abandoned her daughter. No, that just wasn't on at all. I was damaged goods.

14. A CHANGING SCENE

Dublin was buzzing despite the constant news coverage of carnage happening every day across the border in Northern Ireland. The Troubles didn't seem to register all that much in the south. A lot of things in my own life didn't register then either, I suppose. I had battened down the hatches against the unsettling things that life had thrown at me. In truth, the oxygen that really sustained me was theatre.

I found a new teaching position: a permanent and pensionable job, at Emmet Road Vocational School in Inchicore. Both teaching and theatre were now my world. In the evenings I was my other self—a student of drama and a keen observer of the changing world of theatre. I knew every seat in every theatre in town, from the Gods in the Olympia to the plush seats in the Abbey and Peacock, and the long hard wooden benches in the Project and the many basement theatres around the city centre.

It was the early 1970s and the theatre scene in Dublin was changing. The Project Arts Centre, founded by Colm Ó Briain and Jim Fitzgerald, opened its doors to visiting theatre companies from abroad as well as staging new plays. In 1972, Heno Magee's *Hatchet* at the Peacock shocked audiences with its stark and dramatic depiction of working-class life in Dublin. Jim Sheridan's *Mobile Homes* explored new territory in 1976.

One of the biggest sensations was the visit of the Scottish political theatre company 7:84 to the Abbey stage in 1986. They really broke the old dramatic mould of simple kitchen sink drama. While it was exciting to see this transition on stage, I noticed that there wasn't really a similar revolution in the style of dramatic presentation. Vocal projection was poor and acting skills were underdeveloped. It was rare to find ensemble playing anywhere on the stage now except, of course, on the Focus stage. The Abbey did have a school of acting at the time, but the teachers themselves were actors from within the company and were themselves untrained. The only real training ground for actors was still the Focus Theatre.

This was the lens through which I viewed theatre at the time, and because of this I had a vision I wanted to explore. I knew where work was needed and I felt that I could provide that avenue for development. I was on a mission now. The Lantern, in Merrion Square, another basement theatre in another Georgian house, had been in existence under the artistic directorship of Paddy Funge, but had changed the course of its stage practice. The building was near the British Embassy burned down in 1972 in protest at the killing of thirteen people in Derry on Bloody Sunday. As a consequence of this, the Lantern's insurance coverage was raised to such an extent that it could no longer function as a public venue.

The killer clause insisted that the premises could only be used as a private club. Accordingly, instead of staging plays as the Dublin Shakespeare Society did, the Lantern transformed itself into a writers' and actors' workshop. They put out a call for playwrights, actors, directors and artists to join in the workshop. Scripts were exchanged, actors were cast and directors were introduced to playwrights. Every Tuesday night a new play was given a rehearsed reading and presented to a packed audience. After the play, an in-depth Q&A would follow. Very often, theatre critics such as Kane Archer from *The Irish Times* and John Finnegan from *The Evening Herald* appeared in the audience. The lively discussion would continue again around the corner in O'Dwyer's pub on Mount Street, another theatrical bolthole.

When I met the playwright Bernard Farrell, he invited me to direct his first full-length play, *Goodbye Smiler, It's Been Nice*. It was about the ghost of Smiler, who still inhabited the office he once worked in. The script was both funny and serious, a combination that Bernard became famous for. One night in O'Dwyer's, Bernard revealed to us that he was writing a new play based on his time spent in New York, where he had taken part in encounter group sessions.

He explained to us how these groups operated: a facilitator would encourage the group to express their emotions without holding back—to let it all hang out. This did not suit Bernard's shy personality at all, but the playwright in him recognised the solid gold that could be mined from the experience. His play *I Do Not Like Thee, Doctor Fell* was the fruit of those New York sessions. The play was later staged in the Abbey in 1979 and started his relationship with our national theatre.

The Lantern Theatre was the beginning of a new phase in my theatrical life. Some of the actors from my workshop at the Shakes attended, among them Gabriel Byrne and David O'Brien. Both actors read roles in several new plays and became part of the Lantern group. On January 21, 1975, Gabriel's play *Miss Emily*, a monologue written specially for me, was given a rehearsed reading. This wasn't his first foray into writing: he had already written stories for university magazines, reviews for film magazines and pieces for radio.

One night over our post-theatrical pints, David suggested forming our own theatre company. Gabriel came up with the name Bell Productions, after Seán O'Faolain's literary magazine from the 1940s, *The Bell*. The idea was to get away from the usual kitchen-sink plays common to Irish theatre at that time and, as with the Lantern, make new writing our objective. We would stage full productions which would run for several nights.

David took on the task of sourcing new and well-known playwrights. RTÉ producer Seán Walsh had written a one-act play called *Earwig*, a two-hander and a perfect piece for David and Gabriel; in fact, Bell Productions itself became a vehicle for the two actors, who had become good friends by this time.

Rehearsals took place in my Pembroke Road flat, where I applied my Focus training to stretch the acting abilities of the two actors. We improvised off-script. I had Gabriel banging the door of my kitchen so hard at one stage that my neighbour upstairs complained about our unseemly rows and we had to tone it down. We entered into our new roles with such self-belief now that we booked the Players' Theatre in Trinity College for a whole week during their lunchtime summer season. David Storan Byrne joined us as stage manager and Paul O'Brien as our music director.

Seán Walsh, then offered us a second play, *The Dreamers*. We decided to put on both plays as a double bill for the Dublin Theatre Festival that same year, in the same venue. Bell Productions had established itself now, and such was our confidence that we were sure we could go on forever blazing a trail and changing the face of Irish theatre.

Our next production was *Fantology*, a production in the style of a revue—a series of short plays from various playwrights, including Heno Magee, Hugh Leonard, Lee Gallaher, Kevin Grattan, Pascal Finnan, Michael Judge, David Hayes, Donal Foley and Des McInerney.

> *It never dawned on us that there wasn't one woman playwright among our list. Women playwrights weren't in the theatrical ether then. It wasn't until 1991, nearly twenty years later, when myself and Celia De Fréine addressed the subject on the Peacock stage with rehearsed readings by five women writers.*

Des McInerney also designed the poster for the show. It opened in Players on 30th December 1975, running into the first three weeks of 1976. The spectacular set design was created by the sculptor Cecil King, who painted the floor blue and framed the stage in gold leaves. David O'Brien's mother, Betty, was the pianist. David and Gabriel pre-recorded a comedy narrative as a voiceover, separating each scene. We recruited more actors such as Deborah Coulter, the American woman who had played in *The American Dream*, and Ena May, an actress from the Focus Theatre, along with Margaret Gunne and Donal McGuill.

The show received rave reviews and launched Gabriel's career. The initial course of his fame in Dublin followed a clear trajectory from Bell Productions to the Focus Theatre. Ena May introduced Gabriel to the Focus where he acted in a number of plays. His charismatic presence became known to a much wider audience, which eventually led to roles in television dramas.

David also became a professional actor, giving up his job in Irish Lights. David Storan Byrne, our stage manager, later pursued another type of role and became a priest.

While they moved on, I was beginning to realise that, despite all the richness that theatre had brought into my life, it wasn't really for me, at least not on a professional basis. The truth was, I viewed the world of commercial theatre with a certain suspicion; it had yet to prove itself to me, you might say, and I knew that work for a full-time theatre director was always precarious. I knew I could never give it up completely, however, and that it would be possible to continue working with actors and writers in other ways. As a teacher, I could see now that the use of drama in education had much more to offer the world, and I decided redirect my energies in this direction.

One morning, on my way into town to catch a bus to my teaching job, I caught sight of Gabriel as he stepped into a waiting RTÉ pick-up van outside the Shelbourne Hotel. He was on his way to work on the Sunday night drama series *The Riordans*. As the van pulled away, I smiled quietly and thought to myself how our two roads had diverged.

15. PREGNANT AGAIN

Some time after he had left his wife and children and moved in with his new partner, Brian made contact with me. He told me friends of his had seen *Fantology* and had asked him if he knew the director. He said that was when he realised how much he had missed me.

'But you're living with another woman!'

'She's not you, is she?'

And yes, yet again, I was foolish enough to allow these words into my heart, because I still missed him sorely. Despite telling myself over and over again that he was bad for me, my desire to be close to him could and would not be silenced.

He began calling to my flat unannounced, usually late at night, when his new partner was away or otherwise engaged. He would sit in my kitchen using that seductive voice of his to reel me in. He even managed to shed a few tears to show me how much he had missed me. Several more visits took place over the following year until he finally won me over. His steps were carefully calibrated, one at a time. When he mentioned Bronagh, I knew I wanted her back again. If I couldn't have her back, then I wanted to have another baby, just like Bronagh. That was what allowed him back into my bed.

'We were foolish to let her go,' he said as he kissed me, telling me that I was the only woman that he had ever really loved. And again, yet again, I believed him.

Brian called regularly now. When I discovered I was pregnant again, I decided I was going to keep my baby. I had a full-time teaching and I could employ a child-minder. Myself and Brian would welcome this baby into our world together, even though he was still living with another woman. The plan was clear in my head, and this time I wasn't going to hide my pregnancy. I would announce it proudly to the whole world.

My friends welcomed the news and were happy for me. But Brian wasn't at all happy. He didn't even ask me this time if I was I sure he was the father. He didn't ask me anything at all. His expression said it all—blank indifference, bordering on impatience and even repugnance.

One day, I was having lunch with a friend when out of the blue she offered me a pram and a cot in preparation for the new arrival. That was the day that I truly committed to becoming a mother again, even if I would be on my own. I was going into my third month of pregnancy. I was elated, and determined to tell my mother and my siblings this time. But nature had very different plans. When I arrived home after that lunch, I started to bleed. The baby had decided to leave my body, to exit my world.

Immediately I made my way to the National Maternity Hospital in Holles Street and I was taken to theatre for a D&C, then brought back to a ward of women who had their new babies in cots beside their beds. It wasn't long before a social worker was sitting beside me asking questions about my marital status and the name of the father.

When I told her that I was unmarried, all the babies stopped crying, as if to allow their mothers to listen to our conversation. Slowly, I was learning that attitudes to unmarried mothers hadn't really changed that much, not yet.

Another baby lost. Was this God's way of punishing me? Deep down, this was what I felt, though I didn't articulate the idea to myself or anyone else.

> *My second lost opportunity at becoming a mother coincided with a deeply held belief that a woman was more than a womb. Or at least that is what I fooled myself into believing at the time. If I couldn't have*

my own child, then I would help other people's children. A Tarot card reader at the time told me that my students were my family, and so I decided to concentrate on my work as a teacher.

Brian was in the past now. So was Bronagh ,and so was my second lost baby. In the light of this sort of thinking, I buried these experiences as deeply as I could and replaced them with work. It was what you might call a coping strategy but one that, inevitably, drew me away from myself. Nature never forgets. The traces of the umbilical cord leaves its imprint. The tree rings and their hidden narrative like roots gnarled in the soil are always there, waiting to be revealed.

The tribe of nieces and nephews was growing, children of my many brothers and sisters. My siblings disappeared into their own families and I was on the outside looking in. It seemed to me that a woman without children was like a cart without a horse.

During the few months after leaving St Patrick's many years earlier and before I moved into my own flat, I lived with my sister Mary and her husband and children. The household was a busy one, with four young boys. It was thanks to those charming boys that the loss of my baby girl was, for a short period anyway, made bearable. Little by little, I became involved in their lives and became part of their world for a brief time anyway. My friends at this stage had very young children, and I suppose I became a surrogate mother to the growing number of other people's children.

When a flat became vacant in Pembroke Road I moved there and stayed until 1981 when I left Dublin to study Drama in Education with Dorothy Heathcote in Newcastle upon Tyne. It was during this year that my love for drama in education really grew. Before that, however, came my time as a teacher in Emmet Road.

TEACHING

16. EMMET ROAD

Emmet Road, where the Inchicore College of Further Education is now housed, was in my time there a secondary school overseen by the Dublin Vocational Committee (VEC). It educated boys for the Group Certificate, an exam like the Intermediate Certificate but with practical subjects such as metalwork and woodwork. The school's catchment area included some deprived areas: Fatima Mansions, James's Street and Thomas Street.

Looking back, the first-years I taught were my favourite class over my entire teaching career. They were exceptionally talented. My subject was English, with a prescribed set of textbooks. But I wasn't going to be boxed in by words on a page. The world behind the words was the landscape I wanted the boys to experience, and to do that it was necessary for the boys to move out of their desks. To move into drama and into role play.

One boy, Thomas, never spoke. The rest of the class accepted this fact without comment. Nobody put pressure on him at all. Another boy, David, came from a family where both parents were deaf and mute. David was a big Bay City Rollers fan, had a skinhead hairstyle and an earring in one ear. The principal of the school objected to his adornments and demanded his mother come to the school to take her son home. A series of written notes passed between the principal and David's mother until he was eventually allowed back to school in what was deemed acceptable school dress.

I told him that I would find a role for him where he could wear his tartan trousers, Doc Martens and earrings. This happened during a schools drama festival, when I discovered that David attended Irish dancing classes. He was awarded a prize for the most original costume after performing an Irish reel in the Bay City Roller outfit, lifting his elegant feet in those Doc Martens boots.

Role play came naturally to the boys. One day when an improvisation was in progress, Thomas got out of his desk and just joined in without a fuss. He had found his tongue, you might say. At a parent-teacher meeting, I met his father, who revealed that Thomas had witnessed his brother stabbing his mother to death only a few months earlier. Thomas hadn't uttered a word since, cut off from the epicentre of his life in childhood. A pain that was impossible to assuage.

All this was taking place against the emergent drug problem in Dublin. It was now that drugs started to trickle through the local communities. Anything that could distract from the new harsh reality outside was welcome.

Drama was a help. The boys wrote a collection of poems which were illustrated in the art class by Gabrielle, a young woman from Donegal, also a teacher in her first year. I typed out the poems on an Olivetti typewriter and made several copies on the Gestetner machine to make up a book. This little poetry book contained poems about their world, and not the world that the textbooks imposed on them.

Looking back, theVEC was a progressive organisation compared to the private schools and religious-managed schools where, according to my friend Carmel the 'prissy points system' was the ruling force driving the curriculum. Many of our students went on to apprenticeships in trades as plumbers and electricians, setting up their own businesses and giving employment to the next generation of students.

The curriculum wasn't all about exams. The Sports and Cultural Committee was the leading light for extracurricular activities. This committee of teachers from the various schools held meetings in the city to organise inter-school events. Carmel, with whom I had done my HDip and worked in Clogher Road, was also a member. Together we set up an annual inter-schools drama festival adjudicated by well-known theatre people.

Our first festival took place in Crumlin. We invited Jim Sheridan, the playwright and now film director, to adjudicate. It was the early 1970s. That night Gabriel Byrne attended. He was then acting in a play directed by Jim. Carmel's play representing the students from Clogher Road won first place, and David, my own student, won best actor for his interpretation and performance of his Bay City Roller reel.

David couldn't bear to accept the title of best actor; it made him feel self-conscious. 'I don't want to be in your drama class, Miss. Everyone will be looking at me and expecting me to be bleedin great.'

This was another lesson that I learned from this first-year class. Drama was a useful tool in the classroom, as it aided group development. But when a young boy was exposed to personal competition, it violated the vulnerability of the unformed self. It was the teacher's role to protect the student, after all. These boys taught me a lot about how to use drama as a way of exploring physical and emotional literacy.

In 1981 I was granted a year's leave of absence to study with Dorothy Heathcote, drama teacher and academic, at Newcastle upon Tyne University. Michael Keating, then Minister of State at the Department of Education, made it possible for me not only to have the year's leave but with a full-time salary added. He clearly recognised the value of drama in an inner city school.

At an early stage in the one-year course, I had to decide on a topic for my thesis. I couldn't make up my mind, as all the suggestions offered to me were alien to my Irish background. In the end, I decided to base my thesis on Dorothy Heathcote's system of drama, 'Mantle of the Expert.' The final title emerged as '*A theory of education as presented through the drama process Mantle of the Expert.*'

Dorothy's timetable was challenging. She would arrive at her office every day before 7am, and once a week she would invite one of us to engage in a tutorial with her. During these sessions I grew close to her. Dorothy's system of drama was all about endowing the students, as a group, with some special expertise. Her teaching objective was to build the students into experts on a particular topic, step by step. My thesis was based around the Bronze Age, with the students endowed with the expertise of being historians, anthropologists and archaeologists. They were charged with setting up a sociological experiment to see if people today could live in a recreation of a Bronze Age community. Dorothy designed the steps allowing the students to learn. She was the first person I heard mention the concept of ecology.

> *Forty years after completing my degree with Dorothy, my thesis was unearthed by a man called David Allen who, together with Sandra Hesten, catalogued her archive. My thesis was considered the most suitable for examining Dorothy's system. It was written, initially at any rate, because I had difficulty in following her classes. This is not so much a boast, but a reminder that however much a genius like Dorothy Heathcote may be admired, someone else still has to record their system in detail for the rest of the world. And so it was, that in 2022, David invited me to take part in a webinar with drama practitioners from all over the world, to allow me to share my experiences with Dorothy.*

Dorothy's system was born from her belief that the social context and communication systems that operate in any classroom determine the kinds of learning that takes place.

This essential concept was one that informed all my teaching and later filtered into my entire life. The essence of all good relationships is the mode of communication practiced, listening being the most important element in the interaction. Dorothy called this process 'negotiating into meaning'.

Her drama shifted that balance. The Bronze Age project was designed by Dorothy and written up and analysed by me. Dorothy let the students be the agents of communication in the classroom. Her system allowed that to happen. With each step, she created the space for the students—'in role'—to appear as experts in their chosen field.

When I returned to Dublin in 1982, I couldn't help but feel that the city had begun to change. Hard drugs were beginning to take a toll on the young population. And now Aids was lurking around the corner, with disastrous results.

My own life was changing. After I returned from Newcastle upon Tyne, the landlady of my flat in Pembroke Road decided to sell the house. My friend Ruth introduced me to Brendan who was looking for a tenant. It became a relationship of convenience with no real emotional investment on Brendan's part, and I foolishly went along with it. Brendan made me laugh, but he didn't take me seriously.

The relationship wasn't a romantic one even though I did love him. When I moved into his house, he had just lost the love of his life, but it was as if she was still keeping a close eye on him, always in the wings of our relationship. For some time he even kept her framed photograph in the centre of the mantlepiece. He didn't know at the time about my background and the baby. When I eventually told him in 1993, he replied, 'How deceitful of you not to tell me.'

17. PRISON

After returning to my old job in Emmet Road, I found not only had the school changed, but so had my own family home. My youngest sister, Eileen, had upped sticks to Galway with her new husband to start a new life. The world around me had kicked up a gear again, and it was time for me to follow suit.

When a vacancy arose in the prison system, I applied for the job right away. I was interviewed by the head teacher of the prison schools, Vincent Sammon, and the head teacher of St Patrick's, Tom Duffy, who was in charge of the school for young offenders. Tom was a warm, friendly man and I took to him immediately. He had a boyish appearance, smiled a lot and made succinct comments without going into too much unnecessary detail

'You can forget everything you learned about the teaching profession when you enter the doors of St Pat's, Phyl. It's a clean slate here.' I could only guess at what he meant. When I asked him to explain he said simply, 'You'll find out next Monday when you walk through those gates. But we'll go easy on you.'

I was about to learn of the deep chasm between the two worlds, inside and outside the walls. The reality was, and still is, that the majority of the prison population came from areas of terrible deprivation.

There was no curriculum. Nothing was prescribed. The teacher had a blank programme that had to be filled in when the students presented themselves. The needs of the students dictated the programme.

It wasn't as if a fixed number of students enrolled in a prison class either.

It all depended on the number of boys serving sentences. Tom had already told me during the course of the interview that a huge number of students had basic literacy problems. These were students the education system had failed. 'Maybe a subtler, age-appropriate approach could be used to address the gaps in their basic education,' he said.

On Monday morning I headed up the North Circular Road. St Patrick's was an independent part of the prison. It was originally set up in 1956, when the borstal in Clonmel, Co Tipperary, was closed down. I rang the bell on the big, grey metal door. I had the usual bout of stage fright that all first-day teachers suffer from. I knew there would be challenges, problems to solve, but what they might be I had yet to discover.

'Your name, please.' The officer was friendly but direct. He opened another door, which led into the grounds, then pointed me in the direction of the school. A Victorian building with small windows punctuating the grey walls stood in the distance. It looked like a backdrop from a Charles Dickens film. Inside, Tom introduced me in the staffroom. Some of the teachers had video cameras and tape recorders, but my only materials were pen and paper. It was going to be a simple start.

The prison officer brought the boys to the school, a short walk across the yard. Then Tom escorted me to the classroom and introduced me to a group of five boys. The first thing I noticed was that they were all dressed in grey regulation jumpers. They filled up the space in the small room with their bulk. Any one of them could have been a past pupil from Emmet Road or indeed one of my nephews.

Tom nodded towards me. 'This is Phyl. She's now on our team.'

There was a bit of chat about the football match the previous day. 'I see Man United won again.' I was impressed at how natural Tom was with the lads. There was no air of superior authority in his voice. He spoke to them on their own level. As I listened, I thought back to something else he had said during the interview. 'Our lads have all had bad school experiences.'

Tom glanced at his watch. 'Have fun with these guys, Phyl.' The door closed gently behind me.

'What are ya in for?' one of the boys asked.

'That's a nice dress, Phyl,' another said. And then they all started to talk among themselves.

I took a moment to take in the situation. Don't panic, Phyl, I told myself. Don't play the teacher role. These were big boys. I guessed their ages to be around sixteen or seventeen. There was no blackboard, and the only furniture was the table I was sitting behind, and the five desks and chairs. A window at the end of the room gave onto a forlorn-looking patch of grass. It struck me that this little patch of green was the only colour I'd seen since entering; absence of colour is one of the first hints of the senses being deprived. I listened for a while to their chat, like a casual eavesdropper in a cafe. What would I do next?

It felt like that moment on the stage just before an improvisation began, with everyone wondering who would make the first move. There was a knock on the door. My moment of panic was over. I was never so glad to see a prison officer. 'Visit for Paul.'

One down, I thought, and then attempted to take some sort of limited control. 'What do you think you'd like to study in this class?' I knew, as soon as I had spoken, that I had chosen the wrong word.

'Study? Are ya having us on, Phyl?' They began to laugh among themselves. It wasn't so much laughing at me, I knew, but at the whole notion that they came to school to study. School was really a break from the tedium of their confined prison space. It was a means of escape from the prison walls into a new building and an opportunity to meet people 'from the outside.'

They began to interview me now, with one snappy query after another.

'Are ya married, Phyl?'

I thought about Brendan, and my relationship with him. 'No, I'm not married.'

'Do ya have any kids, then?'

This was a question I had always had real difficulty with. Sometimes I said ‘yes,’ when asked by people, because I really had given birth. But I didn’t have a child—my child, that is. Someone else had my child.

‘I have one daughter,’ I said.

‘What age is she?’

‘Sixteen,’

‘Is she a fine thing, like you?’

The fact was, I didn’t know what she looked like. The only image I had of her was from the photo the nuns had sent me and from the memory I held in my heart of her little face when she was six weeks old, the last time I had laid eyes on her.

‘Is this your first teaching job?’

When they found out that I had taught in Inchicore, one of the boys said, ‘I live near there, so I do. Down the road, in Fatima Mansions.’

This was the beginning of a conversation that opened up a whole new landscape of possibilities. One by one, they began to talk about their time in school. They enjoyed talking about themselves. All of them had left school at an early age or had been expelled and left to roam the streets.

‘I’d love you to write something about your favourite local character…just a few words.’ I handed out the copybooks and pens and then sat behind my desk waiting to see what would happen.

‘Can we put our names on these?’

‘Of course you can, you spacer!’ Darren took on the commander-in-chief role.

And then there was a studied silence—at least for a few minutes.

‘How do you spell character, Miss?’

‘She’s Phyl, not Miss.’ Darren spoke again. I saw him now as the watchful minder of his gang. His eyes darted around the room every time he spoke. He was clearly the leader, even though he was the smallest boy. His red hair and freckles gave him a certain presence, despite his size.

‘I’m bleedin’ starvin,’ so I am.’ Jason was rubbing his stomach, which protruded over his waist. I realised that these boys were still growing, and not yet men.

When the bell rang for break, they all left their copybooks on my desk and an officer led them back to the prison and their cells.

In the staffroom at lunchtime, I was to learn that while some of the boys could read, many couldn't. In fact, seventy per cent of the prison population had literacy issues. Although some of the students were enrolled to sit the state exams, this was a rare exception. Only one student was studying for the Leaving Certificate that year.

Over the next few weeks and months, I managed my learning curve carefully and became acquainted with my students. It was very often the case that when a student was making progress, he was released or moved to a different prison, never to be heard of again. I decided therefore to introduce them to as many different learning experiences as possible in the short time available. Of course I introduced drama, and discovered that Darren was not only a good actor but had a compelling voice.

Tom happened to visit the classroom one day when Darren was singing. 'You're better than Luke Kelly!'

Darren's face lit up with a smile that he didn't often show. 'Ah...'

'You should be on the stage.' Tom was genuinely impressed. It was obvious that these lads were not used to being praised or for that matter listened to. This was another learning curve for me.

Dorothy Heathcote's system of drama in education would have a relevance, I thought, to teaching in prisons. Her system was based on endowing the mantle of expertise to the student, thus enabling the person in role the status and power to speak and to be listened to. But I would have to find a way to introduce her system later.

At lunchtime, I told Tom about my drama class at Emmet Road vocational school and about the drama festivals. It wasn't possible to enter these boys into any outside festival, but I wondered about the possibility of bringing a drama group into the prison. Tom nodded in agreement. 'You find a suitable one, Phyl, and I'll do the rest.'

He was as good as his word. The first group we engaged was ACT, the Actors' Contemporary Theatre. This group had been formed by Colette Connor, a theatre director and playwright who had recently returned from London. The play, *Murphy's Law*, was set in Dublin's underworld and followed the escapades of a young man called Murphy who was navigating his way through the world of sex, drugs and crime. The largest room in the school was used so the entire school could attend.

The lads were captivated by the storyline and the authentic voices of the actors. 'They talk just like us,' Darren said, and then he fell silent. What he meant was not only did the actors speak their language but they had the right accent. They weren't actors hamming a Dublin accent.

While I was working in St Pat's my involvement with theatre continued. At this stage I was engaged with the Dublin Youth Theatre. The two worlds came together one day in an oddly unsettling way. The Youth Theatre was founded by Paddy O'Dwyer, and the premises were on Gardiner Street, close to the prison on the North Circular Road. Eilis Mullan, my friend from UCD days and the Dublin Shakespeare Society, was also involved. We facilitated sessions in the Saturday morning drama workshops with students whose ages ranged from fourteen to twenty-two. People like Mia Gallagher, Aidan Gillen, Enda Walsh, Veronica Coburn and Pauline McLynn were part of the workshops.

I arrived one Saturday when an application was being discussed from a prospective member for the Dublin Youth Theatre. Paul was a boy I had known from my classes in St Pat's. He had been seriously smitten with the drama bug and could not only act but had written a very good play about his time in the prison school, in which he sent up the teachers and the prison officers in a touching and amusing way. Paul saw the prison world as a small town and he wrote the piece in the style of *Under Milk Wood.* His title was *Under the Wire.*

The debate ranged from 'What would parents think if we accepted an ex-prisoner?' to 'How could we justify refusing him entry to a drama workshop?' Paul was accepted in the end, but he didn't stay long. It was a case of once a prisoner always a suspect. He told me later on that on one occasion someone in the group had lost their purse and he felt that everyone suspected him of stealing it. He couldn't live with that type of mistrust, so he left. It was only the directors of the youth theatre who knew his story, not the young students. But that didn't matter to him. He still carried the scar of having served time in prison, and it would take time to free himself of that experience. I knew only too well what it was like to carry a scar from your past. It doesn't disappear, it hangs on like a ghost on your shoulder. It was a reminder that we are the sum parts of our past lives.

My ghost was waiting in the wings. But I wasn't to know yet.

Months later, I met Paul at a play in the Project Theatre: a striking young man, dressed in a long dark coat with a smart green scarf draped casually around his neck. He was alone, and his face lit up when he saw me. 'What did you think of the play, Phyl?'

'Not as good as the one you wrote.' The play was set in a London prison but it didn't have Paul's insight or wit.

'Great. But you won't believe what I'm doing now.'

'Tell me...'

'I'm apprenticed to a plumber. I'll be qualified in three years. Better than a prison sentence!'

His story was heartening to hear. I really enjoyed being a part of the enthusiasm of these young men with all of their life in front of them, sorting out which direction they might go in. I often thought of what their dreams were. And of how easily those dreams could be crushed by an uncaring society. In some strange way I felt my life was in parallel with people in prison.

What sort of prison was I in? I asked myself, and who put me there? It was a topic for discussion with myself alone, and only I could answer.

18. AMONG WOMEN

It was customary for teachers to be moved around the prison schools. Accordingly, after two years teaching in St Patrick's, I was moved to the Women's Prison. This didn't involve a geographical relocation; it was the same Victorian building where the lads from St Pat's were imprisoned; in fact, the lads could communicate with the women through the pipes using a sort of coded signal between them. The women's cells were on the first two floors, but the number there was small, with the population amounting to fewer than twenty in the 1980s. It felt like I was moving from a house of teenage boys—which was true—into a house of women around my own age. Like any circle of women, they were a mixed group, and they had a lot to say.

The school was a prefab building outside the prison walls with one large room and two smaller ones. The women who came to classes came because they had chosen to do so. As with the boys, school was a break from the daily routine of sitting in a cell or walking around the yard or doing their laundry. Stealing was their main offence: stealing to support a drug habit, stealing to support a family or stealing simply to stay alive.

One woman called Kathleen stands out in my memory. She was waiflike and tiny. Arriving at the school one morning during my first week of teaching, I discovered her sitting on the ground outside the school door, rolling a cigarette, I smiled at her and said 'Good morning.'

'What's good about it, Fuckface?'

Later she did arrive to some of the classes, but I remember her chiefly because she was one of the four women who died of Aids that year.

During my time there was only one political prisoner. She was serving a twenty-year sentence, the longest imposed on any person in an Irish prison. Most of the women came from deprived areas and had very little education. It was rare that anyone arrived from a middle-class background, although there was one such person who had been sentenced to four years for being a mule for a major Dublin drug baron.

There was a lot of talk during class time, and some voices were louder than others. Sometimes the gathering reminded me of my time around our family table where nobody listened and everyone spoke together. Our mother was only able to listen to one person, and that was the person who spoke the loudest. There was no such thing as taking one's turn. Many of these women were not used to being listened to, and I was acutely aware of such a deprivation in my own personal life. The art of taking turns and listening was a rare skill and one I tried to promote.

Annie was the one who spoke the loudest and with the most authority. Whenever she entered the classroom the other girls stopped talking. The dyed blonde hair may have drained the colour from her face, but the full figure and dominating posture allowed her to commandeer two chairs, one for sitting on and one for extending her posture. She would spread her legs and lean over the back of a chair to ensure nobody else sat beside her.

I overheard a group of women chatting about their men and about how they planned to be more assertive when they were released. Assertiveness was a new buzz concept in the 1980s. Women weren't aggressive, they were assertive, according to the experts anyway.

Annie was certainly assertive. 'My husband thinks he's the boss. He might be the Baron to his friends, but when he's in the gaff, I'm the boss.'

There was silence all around her. Her mates looked at her in awe. 'Good on ya, Annie.' She winked back as much as to say, I know how to handle my man.

'Make sure you're home here for six. That's what I'd say to him, before he went off on his business.' She straightened up her back as she spoke. 'I'd insist that we all sit down at the dinner table together, at least once a day. Oh, yes.' She tapped the table in front of her with her finger to emphasise the point. 'At least once a day.'

Annie had two young girls, but we never found out who was taking care of them. Her husband was serving time down in Portlaoise. It wasn't my business to check the last time that her family sat down together for a meal. Nor did I know when it was likely to happen again. It was never the teacher's business to pry into the nature of either the prison sentence or the crime committed. That was the golden rule.

As compelling as Annie was, I still had to find a way of allowing the other women space to talk. Then I had an idea: if speaking was going to be central to everything, why not start up a debating team? It meant that the women taking part would be listened to and given space to air their views.

I asked Tom if he would allow a team of young men from St Pat's to visit, and if the boys would be even interested. He gave me an upbeat response, of course, laced with a big, broad smile. 'You can have my lads anytime, Phyl. Just name the day and the time.'

The deal was done and a date set. The agreed motion was 'That Drugs Should Be Made Legal'. Our women would propose the motion.

Annie agreed to be the captain of the team. The core of our argument was that if drugs were made legal there would be no drug barons and no stealing, and a decrease in crime would be the result. It was an argument that was gaining ground internationally.

As it happened, Annie never got to air her views and we never got to see how she would perform in front of a new audience. On the morning of the debate, she was called from the classroom. 'Annie, the van is going to Portlaoise, if you want to visit Charlie.' The prison officer smiled kindly at her because he knew she had been asking for this visit for over a month. The next morning she stuck her head into the class to announce that she was giving up debating. She wouldn't be coming to class again.

'Ah, why?' the women all shouted at her. They were genuinely put out now.

'Charlie says I don't need to know how to talk. He says I'm well able to debate on any subject. And if I needed to know anything, to ask him.' She looked at me. 'I'm sorry, Phyl, but he said what would a silly teacher know about the subject anyway?'

Annie never returned to the school. The girls would often tell me snippets about her. They said that she was putting on pounds, stuffing her face all day and asking if she could go to Portlaoise on another visit. One morning, one of the girls came into the class and asked if we had heard the latest news on Annie. She got her visit to the Baron, but he refused to see her. He said she had 'got too bleedin fat.' Told her not to visit him again.

As a teacher, I felt now that I had failed Annie. She had lost faith in herself, as so many of these women had. It was very clear to me that the majority of women's lives were channelled through their men.

And if I was to be truthful, I was no exception. Hadn't I allowed Brian to dictate my emotional life for over a decade? And now I was repeating the same pattern with Brendan, a man who kept me at a distance, a man who was emotionally unavailable to me.

When was I going to be free of needing a man to complete my emotional needs and learn to be an autonomous human being? I remember asking a friend of mine why I kept making the same mistake. Her reply floored me. 'You train people how to treat you Phyl.' And I knew exactly in that precise moment what she meant. I was never able to communicate clearly how bad behaviour affected me. I could never put words on my feelings, and it was only now at this late stage of my life that I was learning how to communicate what I felt.

It dawned on me at that moment that lived experience just cannot be taught, even when distilled into wise advice. It seemed that experience was like the juicy pulp of a fruit, seeping through a time strainer, drop by painful drop.

Rachael, was different from all the other women. She had natural jet-black hair and stood out among the dyed blonde crops. She spoke with a cultured accent and was deeply uncomfortable in a prison setting. The other women shunned her at first, but when it came to the Arts and Crafts class, Rachael helped them to figure out patterns and showed them how to sew and how to assemble a quilt with all the materials that were in the basket. She was an artist to her fingertips.

Her background was unique. Her mother was a poet and teacher and her father was a pioneering psychoanalyst. She had become pregnant at fifteen years of age. Drugs were the common denominator in the prison population and Rachael, as well as being addicted to drugs, had been used and manipulated by the gang leaders of the drug community. On one return trip into Dublin Airport, she was apprehended and sentenced to four years in prison for being found in possession of carrying drugs for a well know drug dealer.

Her two grown-up sons were living with their father but refused to visit her. She had one constant visitor though: her artist boyfriend, who stood by her throughout her prison sentence. He also helped to get her released, further down the line, on health grounds. Rachael often told me stories about him when we were alone in the classroom. How he had tended to her wounds, changing the bandages until she healed, after she had been attacked and her flat set on fire. This man was Graham Knuttel who sadly died on May 27, 2023. His obituary noted, 'You will know that he engaged in life as he engaged in his art—that is to say, boldly and without reserve.'

Making art was encouraged in the prisons. An exhibition of the women's art was held in the recently built ILAC shopping centre. Rachael's bust of a young black woman, sculpted from papier mâché, was the central exhibit. The women weren't allowed attend the opening of the exhibition. I met Graham at the opening and he told me he was actively engaged in researching ways for Rachael's release from prison based on the fact that she had a fragile health condition that was potentially fatal. This legal procedure proved successful.

After her release from prison, she was accepted into the Dun Laoghaire College of Art. There was a solo exhibition of her work at the Apollo Art Gallery in 2005, two years after her death. The centrepiece was a nude portrait of her beloved Graham.

The one political prisoner in the women's prison never attended school and kept to herself for the most part. Her fellow inmates held her in high esteem. Nobody messed with her. She became the first woman prisoner to avail of the Open University programme, a course funded by the Department of Justice. In the 1980s, the prison population were the only ones in the Republic eligible to take these courses. A representative from Northern Ireland would visit her regularly, or one of our teachers would travel to Belfast to discuss her assignments. She did a BA in English Literature and was later allowed to attend Trinity College to complete her HDip. To pass the HDip, a student had to find teaching hours in a second-level school. Happily, a local school gave her hours. To this day, I don't know if the school knew that, after her teaching hours, her journey home took her back to the prison gates, the place that had been her home for the past twenty years. Her husband, who had been sentenced for the same crime, was serving his sentence in Limerick Prison. At one stage of her sentence she had taken a case against the state, claiming the loss of conjugal rights, but with no success.

She passed all her exams and went on to do a Master's degree. One of her projects involved a study of the women characters in Eugene O'Neill's plays. She wrote three monologues relating to this. Only then did she come to the school to ask for assistance from the drama teachers. Myself, Helen Hunt and Maggie Byrne directed her in each of her monologues. The idea of staging the work to a 'real audience' was agreed, but at the last minute the Department of Justice pulled the plug and put a stop to outsiders attending. She was still delighted to perform for the school and the prison staff.

When she was released, we had no idea what life might have in store for her or what plans she had. It was all quite hush-hush and no one asked. Some time after that, when I was transferred to yet another prison school, I was stopped on my way to work by a black-clad figure on a huge motorbike. I did a double take and stepped back a little. The figure wearing the black helmet raised the visor. Her little face appeared inside the helmet. 'How are you Phyl? Just like to say thank you for everything.'

Then she started up that fierce engine and sped away, a happy bird in flight. As I watched the black-clad figure disappear over the horizon, I thought to myself: yes, that's herself...enigmatic to the end with a lot of lost years to be lived.

19. DAVID AND EDDIE

My next placement in the prison school system was in the Training Unit, another building beside Mountjoy Prison. There was yet another bell to ring on yet another oversized grey metal door. I heard the jingle of keys behind the door, which opened slowly. What met my eyes was a surprise: the officer facing me was dressed in civilian clothes.

'Good morning. I'm John and you are very welcome, Phyl.' Over the next few years, our worlds would overlap as we chatted about the world inside and outside of the prison.

The Training Unit was a pre-release centre and housed in a modern building that had something of the appearance of a hotel. The long corridor was bright and the walls were covered with Paul Henry prints of the West of Ireland coastline, scenes of boats and busy fishermen and mountains with cottages. There were visiting rooms on either side. But there was also an inescapable smell of Jeyes Fluid. When I went up the stairs to see where the school was, I looked out from a landing window onto four grey walls crowned with barbed wire. This was still prison territory. That much was very clear.

During my first week there,Arts Week was in progress. Bernie Masterson, the arts teacher there at the time, who is now an artist and a film maker, was responsible for introducing the idea, later adopted by the other prison schools. Artists, writers, dancers and lecturers were invited to give workshops and performances. The group that surprised me most of all was the Irish Ballet Company.

'Ballet. Are ya mad Phyl. That's only for sissies.'

There was a wall of prejudice from the men when the company first arrived in the gym. But before they asked anyone to dance, the troupe put the men through their own exercise regime. With sweat and strain came respect. And when the men heard that the Irish rugby team—all big, bulky lads—had been trained by their ballet master, resistance evaporated. The next step was to learn a few ballet moves and lifts, and then to practise. The men began to see it as a physical workout. When this visiting company eventually came to dance, the men looked at the performance with new eyes.

My own brief as a teacher was to engage in the area of literacy, literature and drama. As I had recently qualified as a yoga teacher, I was also given permission to teach it to any willing students. After a few yoga sessions with a number of lads, Ted, a man from the midlands, entered the room. 'I can do cartwheels! Watch!'

I sensed immediately that he was different from the others, a little child-like, maybe, but a gentle soul. He had a mop of curly hair and an enthusiastic smile. I guessed he must be in his early forties. Before I could answer, he was on his hands, his feet high up in the air. This wasn't safe practice, but there was nothing much I could do about it. Ted returned to the class later on and engaged in many of the yoga postures we were doing. His favourite was the Warrior Pose. Much later, I learned that he was in prison for shooting dead his next-door neighbour who had bullied him and had been attempting to steal some of his livestock. Ted had been left to run the farm alone after his parents' death and felt deeply responsible for its continuity.

By now, I had come to understand that my job was to recognise the needs of the students. The number one need was literacy in all its forms, including emotional and social literacy. Even though the men's offences were of no concern to the teachers, sometimes, however, because of media coverage, there would be a visitor in the class whose story was in the public domain.

David's story was now an open book. He spoke with a cultivated accent. He was tall and striking-looking, with a brown head of hair like a halo around his head. A well-trimmed beard completed the picture of academic detachment.

He asked me one day if he could use the computer in the corner of my room, promising not to interrupt the class. It was common for students to pop in and out of classes. When David settled himself down in front of the computer, I continued on with my two students.

One was at the end of a ten-year sentence and was fixated on learning how to do 'attached writing.' He had never mastered joining up his letters, having left school at the age of ten. His big, broad hands grasped the thin biro firmly as if it was a dangerous tool that had to be controlled. The tattooed muscles on his arms pulsated as he moved the biro across the page. The contrast with the man at the keyboard was crystal clear. Both similar ages but from different backgrounds, different sides of the social track but now sharing the same destination.

During my HDip days I remember a visiting lecturer making the point that all babies in their cradles in the maternity ward were equal. The differences only emerged as soon as the parents brought the babies home. The location of the household governed the child's development.

As a teacher, I had to be very careful not to undermine the confidence of any student. As Dorothy Heathcote used to say, 'Never confront a student with their own ignorance, and always protect their self-image.' A man's reading age might be at the level of a five-year-old, but his life experience was another matter. Age-appropriate reading material was crucial, and that related as much to subject matter as it did to language.

During the course of one conversation on exploring a suitable theme, another visitor arrived in the classroom. This time it was Eddie.

'Good morning, Phyl.' He was holding a sweeping brush and was in the middle of his morning clean-up duties.

'How's it goin lads?'

He looked over in the corner at David. The two men nodded at each other silently. Eddie had a skinhead haircut, a slight turn in his blue eyes and a very pale complexion.

'We were talking about programmes on telly,' one of the lads at the table said.

'The only thing I do watch is boxing.' Eddie jabbed the air with a powerful hook.

He swung at an imaginary sparring partner. 'I tape all the fights and I keep all me videos in me room in the gaff.' Eddie wasn't interested in learning how to read or write. His videos were colour-coded, and he knew exactly what each colour represented. He was able to organise what needed to be ordered in his own world. He never ignored the people sitting at the tables, and would sometimes pretend to study what the men were writing or reading.

'Good luck to yiz! Gave up on all of that stuff years ago, so I did. I have me own way of remembering, so I have.' He tapped his temple with his finger then looked around the room in the direction of David. 'What do ya think, over there?'

David stretched his long back and smiled gently. 'Whatever gets you by.'

Eddie gave him the thumbs-up. 'That's what the teacher in Sheriff Street used to say to me.'

He turned back to the other two men. 'Do ya remember the Lyon's Tea ad on the telly? The Black and White Minstrels dancing across the place?' He mimed a Bojangles dance across the room, up as far as David, and sang 'Lyons Tea, da, da, da, da, da...' when he reached him.

There was a round of applause and laughter. Pleased with himself, he left the room with a big smile on his face. This was Eddie. Every morning he'd drop in and entertain us before moving on to his next job. This continued for the remainder of his sentence. Coming towards his last few days inside, he made his final visit to the room. That day, without any advance notice, David stood up from his computer and presented Eddie with an illustrated, typed edition of all the stories he had told us, including the one about his school days in Sheriff

Street, with the Black and White Minstrels dancing across the page.

'Ya mean to say ya were listening to me all the time?' Eddie spoke with a mixture of astonishment and emotion and was near to tears. He turned over the pages and held open the drawing of the Black and White Minstrels. 'Those are all me words too?'

'Word for word, Eddie.'

Yes, I could truly say that Eddie was one of the most emotionally literate men I knew. He left the room for the last time that day with the book of his words in his hands. We had made a few copies of the book for Eddie's release date. Of course, nobody had suspected that David had been typing this book all the time. He had kept it well hidden. David himself was a man who knew so much about books and art. A solitary, quiet soul who didn't miss a beat. It had been a meeting of minds, on the part of the two men. Both worlds apart. But for the time spent in prison they were part of a family, and I felt part of that family too.

20. DRAMA AND DEBATING

After a few years in the Training Unit, in response to student needs, I started to introduce drama and public speaking. A search for scripts was pretty useless because there was nothing really age-appropriate around, so I decided to write my own plays.

I invited the playwright and poet Celia de Fréine to join me, and the City of Dublin Vocational Educational Committee offered us a grant. Sarsfield Press's 1990 publication of our book, *Literacy, Language and Role Play,* coincided with International Literacy Year.

One memory of the night of the publication party at the Teachers' Club in Parnell Square was of hearing the loud applause coming from the bar as we were leaving. They were cheering the announcement on television of the release of the Birmingham Six after sixteen years in prison for a mass murder in which they had played no part.

The following year, Celia and I were awarded an Arts Council Grant to look at the state of female playwrights and we called our small group of writers 'The Women Playwrights' Forum.' During this period women playwrights tended to channel the voices of historical female figures to express their dramatic view-point. It was rare that a woman writer used her own personal voice to explore current issues. Irish theatre was not ready yet for such a voice to be heard. Of course, there were exceptions like Maeve Binchy and before her Maura Laverty and Máiréad Ní Grádha, but I have written previously on this subject and will not go into detail here. We chose five playwrights: Ivy Bannister, Leland Bardwell (sadly deceased in 2016), Colette Connor, Celia de Fréine and Clairr O'Connor. A grant of £2000 was awarded to us. Our project was to present rehearsed readings followed by a Q&A. The title of the event was 'Women at the Peacock.' This happened in June, 1991. The artistic director at the time was Garry Hynes and her literary editor was Fintan O'Toole. Sad to say, none of the playwrights were offered a full production at the Abbey.

In 2015 Fiach Mac Conghall, then artistic director, announced the 2016 programme, entitled 'Waking the Nation,' commemorating the Easter Rising of 1916. All the plays were by men, except for one play for children written by Ali White. The result of this exclusion of women writers was 'Waking the Feminists,' born to ensure that women's voices would be heard.

I do regret deeply that we omitted from our group of five women writers a very important playwright at the time called Miriam Gallagher, who sadly died in 2018. I first became acquainted with her while I was babysitting her children during my UCD student days. Over the years we became friends, and as time went on she joined the Dublin Shakespeare where I cast her as Gertrude in my production of *Hamlet* in 1980. She also began writing for the stage with works based on the lives of historical figures like the Gore Booth sisters, but she was one of the few women playwrights at the time to evolve into mainstream writing. In 1983 her play *Fancy Footwork* was performed in the Focus as part of the Dublin Theatre Festival. It was commissioned by EXIT (Mountjoy Prisoners' Theatre) directed by Claire Wilson (now Claire Galligan) and featured professional actor Fidelma O'Dowda along with members of EXIT. In 1984, I directed her play *Dreamkeeper* for the Dublin Theatre Festival performed in The Damer theatre. A collection of her plays, *Fancy Footwork*, was published in 1991 in association with the Society of Irish Playwrights.

Looking back now, I do remember that Mia Gallagher, her daughter, directed Lia Bardwell's play *Jocasta*, the Greek myth written from a feminist perspective, as part of the Peacock readings of women playwrights. Mia is a very successful novelist and hopefully will bring her mother's plays back to life again.

My friend Carmel, who was still teaching in Clogher Road, asked me to judge an annual public speaking event she had organised in Ballyfermot College. It was like an Oscars ceremony, with all the speakers dressed up to the nines, the girls in evening dresses and the boys in tuxedos. As a judge, it was fascinating to discover the topics raised and the different levels of student contribution.

This sort of thing wasn't available to our prison students. But why not try something like it? Carmel herself was the person who waved the magic wand and made it happen. Several times over the course of a year, various colleges would visit.

Towards the end of each year, a final was hosted by the Training Unit, with an invited panel of judges. The newscaster Anne Doyle (who had herself been an all-Ireland debating champion during her school days) chaired one year, and on other years Jonathan Philbin Bowman and Nell McCafferty. To our surprise, Nell commented on the fact that the panel of judges were all women.

The year that Anne Doyle chaired the final ended with a group of us gathering in a local pub. Anne remarked, 'You know, we were much better in our day.'

We all looked at her questioningly.

'We spoke from the heart, then. Just like those young guys in there tonight.'

I knew what she meant. It seemed to me too that many of the speakers coming from outside were cosmetically coached to a polished and over-rehearsed performance. That isn't to say that they weren't good, but there was a marked difference between the styles of delivery. Our men had real passion and belief in what they were saying. The reality was that the men were talking from their own lived experiences.

Drama and public speaking became the core of the men's curriculum—and, of course, literacy. A drama script proved valuable for the literacy classes, as the page layout was relieved by white space, and the use of improvisation allowed for expression and reflection. Sometimes I would record the dialogue created by the men, type it up and use it as literacy material in the class.

Then one group of men began showing an interest in drama for its own sake. And towards the end of the 1980s, Michael Campion, a radio producer from RTÉ, invited me to enter my group into the P J O'Connor radio drama competition. He had a script in mind about a group of young footballers training for a championship. Unfortunately, I cannot remember the name of the playwright, nor do RTÉ have any record of it in their archives.

In those days, entries were the actual performances of the drama and not the script itself. And I had a ready-made cast in my drama group. As with any group, there were personalities who were far more dominant than others. It was a real challenge for me to find the right cast for the play. The lesson here, I decided, was to show that there was no such thing as a small part. That every part was important, in its own way.

An RTÉ crew came into the prison to record the play for the radio broadcast, but the lads weren't allowed to attend the awards ceremony in Donnybrook. The head teacher from the Training Unit attended with me, and the lads were delighted when they learned that we had won the award for Best Production.

The occasion was significant for me too, but not in a positive way. The producer of the awards ceremony was Brian, who had moved from theatre to radio. He never left his workstation once throughout the ceremony, so we did not communicate. Little did either of us know then that we would have reason to meet soon over an entirely different matter.

The day I left the prison service, June 26, 1996, was a sadly momentous one: the day that the campaigning journalist Veronica Guerin was shot dead, murdered in her car while stopped at a traffic light at Newlands Cross in West Dublin.

Ten years was a long time to teach in the prisons, and now I felt the need to broaden my horizons. I had learned so much from teaching in prison. Of how we as a society had let down so many of our students during their growing years. But my teaching career was not quite over, as I had decided to stretch myself in a different environment.

21. LIBERTIES COLLEGE

The red bricks of the Victorian building sang out a song of history. This was old Dublin, part of the Iveagh Buildings complex formerly owned by the Guinness brewing dynasty. In 1976 the Dublin Vocational Educational Committee bought it, and the school was officially named Liberties College of Further Education.

At the top of a large room, the principal Michael King was ready to conduct the first staff meeting of the term. He was a handsome man, dark with deep blue eyes and the magnetism of a film star. I immediately took to him. It was like being in a theatre, with every row in the room filled with colourful people of different ages. I couldn't wait to hear what was about to emerge.

After a while I heard the words, 'Welcome to our new staff member, Phyl, who has recently got out of prison.' There was a chorus of laughter, and I immediately knew I had arrived at the right place.

The pastoral care programme for the students was all-embracing; the staff looked after the students as if they were all part of a large family. The philosophy of the VEC schools, as they were known then was to give poor kids a chance. The Leaving Certificate wasn't the end goal. As Carmel from Clogher Road remarked, 'The tyranny of the prissy points system isn't the ruling endgame.'

Liberties College was one of the first schools to introduce the Leaving Cert Applied (LCA) where students were taught practical skills. They also had a rich Post Leaving Certificate (PLC) programme. I taught at both levels.

Two teachers stand out in my memory: Loretto Wrynne and Anne Weber. Both were role models whose work extended into the community, to places like Oliver Bond flats, Fatima Mansion and School Street, and to the Iveagh Hostel for homeless men. Anne was also in charge of the Outdoor Pursuits programme where students were taken up the mountains. For some of them it was their first time to set foot outside of the city. On one of these occasions I was part of the group, and on our return, Anne's daughter Gráinne was on the steps of the college to meet her mother. She was holding her six-week-old baby in a pouch on her chest, and when I looked into the child's face I was completely immersed in that baby scent, which transported me back to Bronagh. A pure body memory reaction on my part, I immediately felt the warmth of my baby on my chest and I was back in that nursery in 1967. The years had moved on quickly, far too quickly, but she was still imprinted in my heart even though I had no idea what part of the world she was in.

It was during these years that I finally separated from Brendan. We were not good for each other, and it took me a long time to realise that two people are needed in one relationship. I had attended family weddings, christenings, birthdays, but I was always the one who arrived alone, the one without a partner, even though I was still living with Brendan during those years.

In Ireland, the family is the unit that matters. Few people acknowledge the life of the single person. It's as if having no children to talk about means you are a failure. Well, something like that. Conversations at family gatherings dwell on family matters. But, as Shakespeare said, 'There is a world elsewhere'—and that's the one I wanted to dwell in.

My time in Liberties College was the happiest of my entire teaching experience. It was when I unfolded both as a teacher and as a person. I felt as if I had come home, I had found my tribe. The group of women teachers in that college were women who could have ruled the country, and Michael King could have been our Taoiseach. He was a man of enormous integrity who worked for the good of the college and was fair to all of his staff and students.

I took early retirement from Liberties College in 2005, but I learned fairly quickly that a life of doing little would not suit me. A new beginning was necessary. It wasn't that I didn't already know how life could take a sudden and unexpected swerve and present one with unexpected challenges. That is exactly what had happened when a letter came through my front door in June 1993. It was a new beginning that I had hardly dared to dream of.

ELIZABETH

22. A LETTER

1993

One bright, sunny morning (as many fairy tales begin) the postman delivered a letter written on a small piece of paper, notebook size. But there was nothing small about the impact it had. The letter was dated June 28, 1993, and it was from the Eastern Health Board.

> *Dear Ms Herbert,*
> *Our records show that you gave birth to a baby girl in St Patrick's Mother and Baby Home on the 18th July, 1967...Please phone our office at your convenience in order to make an appointment with the undersigned...*

It was signed by someone called James.

This was a letter I had dreamed of receiving. But I had never dared to believe it would ever arrive. A friend of mine who had recently adopted a baby girl from another country had spoken to me about how difficult it would be for her daughter to trace her birth mother when she became an adult. She urged me to ensure that the health authorities always had my current contact details.

I knew St Patrick's had my parents' address, because, twenty-six years earlier a nun there had sent me the photo of my smiling baby in her pram, the photo that had assured me she was in a happy home. And there was also the letter that had invited me to attend the solicitor's office to 'extinguish my rights' as Bronagh's natural mother.

I did as my friend suggested and passed on my change of address, and said that I was in the process of moving again from my last address. I had already moved by the time the appointment to meet the social worker was made. He invited me to his office on July 5, 1993, a date, like all the dates associated with my daughter, that became etched in my memory.

On the day, I cycled to the Eastern Health Board Community Care Centre in Clonskeagh, from which James, a social worker, James had sent the letter. James was a very young man, probably not much older than Bronagh. He was respectful of my feelings. He explained to me that the Eastern Health Board didn't actually have a tracing policy, and that it was only by accident that he had encountered the file containing our details. He had one piece of shocking news: my daughter had been looking for me for eight years. This was the first time that anyone had acted on her letter.

James made me a cup of tea, making sure that I was in a relaxed state for our meeting. He had read my letter and the letter written by my daughter seeking details of her birth mother. (Months later, he told me that his own mother had died giving birth to him and that he had always wished he could have met her. He felt he had now realised that dream by proxy, as you might say, through my meeting with Bronagh.)

'I have made contact with your daughter,' James said.

I couldn't lift the cup of tea to my mouth. Was he really saying what I had heard?

'You actually spoke to her, you mean?'

My hand automatically went up to my chest where I had Bronagh's baby photo in my blouse pocket.

He paused a moment. I stared hard at his mouth, willing more precious words to pour out. Words that would comfort me. Words that might, ultimately, lead me to my daughter.

'We only spoke on the phone,' he said. 'But I'll be in a position shortly to tell you more, after I meet her in person.'

'You will be actually meeting her?' My voice rose into a louder register, and I have to say that I was a little put out by the fact that this stranger, however nice and well-meaning he was, would be meeting my daughter before me.

'And when will that be?' I sat back in the chair and took a deep breath. This was an awful lot of reality to take in.

'Very soon. We have to confirm things. Would you like to know what she is called now?'

'Oh yes.' I held my breath in anticipation.

'I'm not at liberty to tell you her surname yet, but her first name is Elizabeth.'

'Elizabeth...' I exhaled and repeated the name, and repeated it again, sounding out the four syllables as though it were a completely new word to me. I could feel a wave sweeping over my entire body, a sort of tingling. I was back in St Patrick's now, holding her in my arms in that circle of mothers and babies, cooing and feeding. I was in that room again with Bronagh in my arms.

'Would you like a tissue?' James watched me carefully, smiling all the time.

I wanted him to tell me more, much more. Where was she now? And did she really want to meet me?

He told me that she was the manager of a large office in Galway and that she held a very responsible position there. The nuns had told me that her adoptive family lived in the midlands. James continued. 'Elizabeth is a very assertive person. She wasn't at all happy with the way my department ignored the letter she wrote when she was eighteen.'

My eyes refocused on James. 'So she really wants to meet me, in other words?'

'Oh yes. But first I will arrange a meeting with her in Dublin to set everything up.'

'And when can I meet her? And where?'

'That's exactly what we will be discussing.'

I cycled home from James's office that July afternoon feeling like I was floating on some sort of angelic vibration—a sacred breeze guiding me to reunification with my long-lost daughter. It was a miracle. The photo of the smiling face of my baby girl was glowing in my pocket.

That July evening I was sitting in the Gate Theatre with my friend Celia, waiting for the curtain to go up on *A Midsummer's Night Dream*, when I thought to myself: this is what this is, a dream come true in the middle of summer. My mind wasn't on the play in front of me. It kept floating back to Bronagh's father reading a Shakespearian sonnet to me in his liquid cello voice during those heady days when we first met.

> *Shall I compare thee to a summer's day?*
> *Thou art more lovely and more temperate...*

I thought Brian meant every word then. I believed him. It was my first experience of love and desire, and Brian was everything I desired. Of course, I didn't realise then that I would spend a lifetime carrying the fruit of our short time together. Shakespeare, no doubt, would have known what was to come.

> *Rough winds do shake the darling buds of May*
> *And summer's lease hath all too short a date.*

It had taken me ten years and more to accept that my relationship with Brian was over. The final death blow to my passion was the day he ignored my second pregnancy, showing no compassion at all for the miscarriage of our baby. Was it ten wasted years? How could I answer such a question when Bronagh was the result of our relationship? I do know, though, that I shunned many a good man because of my passion for him. And no one person could replace him, such was my obsession. The heart wants what the heart desires.

But on this balmy midsummer's night I was full of hope and dreams.

The next day I phoned Carmel to tell her. She was one of the few friends who knew my story. She celebrated Bronagh's birthday with me every year in her house where her two small boys played around us. We talked about her, wished her well in life from a silent distance, and wondered where and how she was.

Carmel bundled her young sons into the car after my phone call and drove to meet me in the Swan shopping centre in Rathmines. Her two boys sat at a table nearby, knowing that there was something big being discussed. They would have heard Bronagh's name every year on her birthday being mentioned by their mother as we both spoke about her in hushed tones at their kitchen table. On the way home, the older boy who was thirteen, asked Carmel what the special news was. When she told him, he said simply, 'But your mother is always your mother. The one you knew since you were a baby. The one who knows you best. You can't have two mothers.' Time would prove the worldly wisdom of this young boy's words.

Twenty-six years is a long time to keep a secret from your family. I decided that I should visit my mother and read Bronagh's letter to her as a way of breaking the news. My brother Noel, who was living with my mother, would also be in the house. I phoned to prepare them. 'I have something to tell you. You might get a shock when you hear.'

When I began to read the letter aloud to them, I broke down halfway through. It was too much for me. My brother took the letter from me and continued reading. My mother listened in sympathetic silence. As I was leaving the house, she finally spoke. 'You must have thought I was a terrible mother that you couldn't tell me?'

'No, I didn't at all. But I just couldn't face telling anyone in the house.'

I rang RTÉ the next day, despite my misgivings. When Brian answered the phone his first words were, 'You've found her.' It had been a long time since we had last been in touch, despite the fact that he must have seen me at the Awards Ceremony in RTÉ a short time previously. He immediately came around to my place and we spent the night together. Afterwards, he sent me a card, which said, 'Still Love you After all this Time.'

I was in Kerry visiting my friends Fíona and Paddy when I spoke to James again. He had made an appointment for me to phone him to find out the results of his meeting with Elizabeth. Even though Fíona and Paddy knew Brian, they had no idea of my involvement with him. Before I travelled down to Kerry, I told them that I had something special to tell them.

On my first evening in Kerry, the appointed time for my phone call with James arrived. It was before dinner. The public phone box on the seafront was a short walk to the village. The wide, wild Atlantic was rushing in towards the road as I walked to the kiosk. I put in my coins, rang the number and James answered. As he spoke, his words built an image of a girl who was now an adult. Who had been out there in the world, with no connection to me, until a few days ago.

James clarified a few of the previous facts I had been told. My daughter was not a manager in an office. She hadn't grown up in the midlands. She was a lecturer in a university and had grown up in Galway. This false information was given to protect the anonymity of Elizabeth until both parties agreed to share specific information. 'A very articulate young woman.' James kept repeating this fact as though it was of some significance. I drank in every word he said. But his final words threw me a little. 'I'll visit you at your new address next week. Then we can confirm the arrangement for the meeting.'

I wondered afterwards why he didn't arrange this on the phone, but the truth was that he wanted to observe my living circumstances at first hand before the meeting.

Walking back to my friends' house and watching the mighty waves crashing on the beach, I felt the universe was in harmony with me. The waves themselves were dancing with joy at my news. I was about to meet my daughter at long last. I wanted to catch a wave to remind me of this moment. But catching a wave was about as likely as picking up the phone again to talk directly to Elizabeth.

When I arrived back to the house, Fíona was preparing dinner in the kitchen. I watched her nervously as she prepared the vegetables for the stir fry. She is a superb cook, and every time I visit I come away with another new recipe.

'Guess who I was talking to on the phone?'

She smiled over at me. 'I don't know. Why didn't you use our phone in the living room?' I watched her as she dried her hands.

'Who were you talking to then, that was so private?' She gave a little laugh; she obviously felt there was something strange about my behaviour.

'Well...' I stuttered, and then I gasped out the words. 'I was finding out about the identity and whereabouts of my baby.'

'Is this another play you're involved in, Phyl?'

Paddy arrived in from the garden then with a bucket of newly dug potatoes. Fíona looked at him and said, 'Phyl has a story to tell us, Paddy.'

'It's not a story Fíona. It's fact.'

When I named the father they looked at one another in astonishment. 'How come you've kept this information to yourself for so long?'

'I was ashamed to tell you. That's why. After all, Brian was married. I thought you'd be horrified.'

Nobody seemed to know what to say. 'I'd have married you myself, Phyl, if I thought you could have kept your child.' Paddy then looked at Fíona, 'You know what I mean, love.'

Fíona smiled and said, 'Brian always had a reputation for playing away from home, but it was never serious. Not like this.'

I wanted to know more about their relationship with Brian. What they really thought of him. Both Fíona and Paddy were fluent Irish speakers and had been involved in that part of Brian's world.

'I was in his play. It was the year I started UCD,' Paddy says.

'The one that lasted one night only?' Fiona asks.

Fíona explained that Brian had pulled the play after the opening night. Ernest Blythe, managing director of the Abbey Theatre, had sanitised his bawdy version of Flann O'Brien's novel *An Béal Bocht*. Brian's free-spirited version involved singing and dancing. Blythe had bowdlerised it without informing him. But

Brian wasn't having any interference with his script, so he cancelled the show.

I knew that his adaptation of *An Béal Bocht* had opened the Peacock Theatre but I didn't realise it had been taken off after the opening night. 'When did it open, then?'

Paddy thought for a moment. 'I think we have the poster somewhere.'

Fíona scoured the bookshelves and found it on the top shelf. 'It was the 18th of July, 1967. We kept it for its historical interest. The Peacock was to be a new Irish language theatre.'

'The 18th of July, 1967?' I said in surprise. 'That was the same date my baby girl was born.'

Paddy put his arm around me. 'It wasn't the only drama in his life on that date, so.'

'It must have been awful to lose your baby, Phyl. How did you manage to keep all of that to yourself?' Fiona rolled up the poster and left it back.

I sat down to dinner with my friends, feeling that a heavy cloud had lifted. That night, as I lay awake in bed, I thought to myself once more that no one really knows anyone else fully. Maybe we don't even know ourselves.

I was glad I had told my friends, but I realised, at the same time, that it must have been quite a shock for them.

An old story came into my mind. My mother had this wonderful woman friend for most of her married life, Mrs Downey. After this woman's death, I found out something unusual about her story. Baffling, even. I remember saying to my mother, 'That would never happen with any of my friends.'

Mrs Downey had a large family. But what I learned after she died was that she hadn't given birth to the three eldest children. Her story was that after dating a widower for a short time, he had proposed to her. There was no honeymoon, but was not that unusual in those days. He brought her instead to his house for the first time under the pretext of having the wedding breakfast in the home that was about to be hers. As he put the key in the door, he declined to lift his new bride over the threshold. Why? Because his three small children ran into his arms. 'Here's your new mammy,' he said. It was the first time she had heard of his three little secrets.

Before our first meeting James suggested that Elizabeth and I exchange photos and letters with some information about ourselves. This seemed a sensible enough idea. But I had an image in my head of what she might look like now. I'm embarrassed to say that I was hoping for a younger version of myself.

I searched all my photo boxes to find a suitable one. Certain facts had to be faced: the body changes over twenty-six years, and the mind persists in holding on to images of our younger selves. Those Russian Matryoshka dolls were in my mind as I opened one photo box after the other, trying to avoid the present tense, trying to roll back the years to reveal a younger, slimmer version of myself. The weight I had piled on, especially after giving up smoking in 1986, wasn't an image I particularly wanted Elizabeth to see.

There were very few photos of me by myself, except for one on a tennis court, wearing a short white skirt. 'Mutton dressed as lamb' would have been a suitable caption. What was I thinking? Hoping to find a photo of myself where I was young and pretty? Oh, if only I could roll back those years! The one I liked in the end, and the one that actually flattered me, had been taken in a garden in London on one of my summer trips. There was another person in it beside me, but it was a good photo, one where I wasn't posing. And I liked the colourful dress I was wearing.

The letter was another matter. It was the hardest one I have ever had to write. I had to dig deep into my very bones to pull out a part of me that might be acceptable to this girl I had given birth to— and abandoned—when she was only six weeks old. Of course, I didn't see it like that at the time. I thought I was setting her free and saving her from a hostile environment.

This letter wasn't the place to explain the complexity of leaving a child in 1967. It was more of a pen portrait of myself and my present world. I told her that I was single, that I had separated from my partner, had no children and lived alone. Of course I told her I was a teacher and had a big interest in theatre.

After all, I didn't want to appear like a pathetic, lonely woman.

James told me when to expect my daughter's letter. It would arrive on the midday post. That day, as I was still teaching in Mountjoy Training Unit, I couldn't wait until the evening, so I asked Bernie Masterson, the art teacher, to drive me back to my house in Sandymount at lunchtime, so eager was I to receive the letter.

I unsealed the envelope and took out a number of photos of a girl in a wine jacket draped over a snow-white blouse. The wide sea was behind her and her short hair was gleaming in the sun. I was taken aback when I looked at the photos. The first person that entered my mind when I saw her beautiful face was Brian. I wasn't at all pleased.

The notepaper was a lovely shade of cream and the writing was neat and consistent. I knew before reading her words that I liked her. 'I have an older brother and sister...' This was interesting to me, as I wondered how those siblings had bonded with a new baby coming to their house. It would be one of the many questions I would ask Elizabeth when we finally met. But the real detail that surprised me was that she had rented a flat as a student on Palmerston Road, minutes away from where I then lived on Cowper Road. We might both have been passengers on the bus which stopped outside her house. I thought of all the times we might have met, standing there in the early mornings at the same bus stop, our lives going in different directions.

I was close to tears for the missing moments and minutes and years, worn away by the passage of time. And I promised I would make up for every minute of it.

23. FIRST MEETING

It is Saturday, 2nd of October, 1993. The time is 2.30pm. The place: the Davenport Hotel, Dublin.

What do I say to her when we meet? Do I hug her? No, that would be too invasive altogether. This girl doesn't know me and I don't know her. The fact that I did know her intimately for the first six weeks of her twenty-six years doesn't give me permission to assume any degree of familiarity. I will hand over the first moments to her. I will let her lead and I will follow.

I allowed myself to think a lot about what I would wear for this first meeting. I desperately wanted to present myself in the best light possible. A well fitted blue trouser suit and a white blouse, all bought for the occasion, would look suitably understated. Black ankle boots rimmed with a red trim would soften the business-like image.

I set off to meet my daughter. James had told me that the correct term now was 'birth daughter.' I was uncomfortable with it at first, but now I understand the usage better. After all, I had only known Elizabeth for those precious few weeks. My part in her life had been to give birth to her, to bring her into a safe environment. Then to set her off on the river of life.

How would she view what I had done to her? A thousand questions were bubbling up inside me, demanding answers. What sort of life did she live? What were her parents like? Did she have good friends, and was she in a relationship? I knew, ultimately, that I would have to silence my curiosity for the moment.

Just allow Elizabeth to share whatever came naturally to her.

It is a sunny day as I walk through the doors, my first time ever to visit this new Dublin hotel. I immediately regret not having paid a visit earlier to familiarise myself with the surroundings. The marble floor at the reception area shimmers like water at low tide, and the sound of my new boots on this hard surface sends a shock through my body. The next few steps feel like wading through an incoming tidal wave. For a moment I think I have lost my footing.

And then I see her. She is sitting with James. I had completely forgotten—how did I do that?—that he would be here for the initial introduction. He is sitting with his back to me, facing her. Elizabeth is looking straight at me with a piercing gaze which says, *Who is this woman coming towards me?*

James stands up and steps backwards, allowing me to come nearer. It is like walking into a magnetic field—an invisible ley line marking the place between us. The words exchanged in those first few seconds don't register at all. Words don't seem to matter now, because, for those first few moments, I am in a place above mere language. We are looking at each other now for the first time in twenty-six years.

James glances from me to Elizabeth. Then, after a quick greeting he takes his leave and exits slowly.

'How are you?' Elizabeth looks at me carefully, taking in the features of my face. A slow smile spreads across her beautiful mouth, lighting up those clear blue eyes. 'I'll order. Tea or coffee?'

My stomach is churning. 'Tea, please.'

The waitress brings the tea and sets the tray down gently in front of us. A ray of sunshine beams over the head of the young woman opposite me. I study her slender hands as she pours the tea. I need to say something but I feel tongue-tied. Every word that rises up in my throat I push down again. I take a deep, calming breath. 'So, when did you arrive in Dublin?'

Elizabeth takes a sip of tea. 'Yesterday. My brother and his family live near you, actually.'

Suddenly, the noise of massed male voices around us swamps our words. A group of people have gathered to watch an international rugby match.

'Let's go somewhere else,' Elizabeth says.

'Good idea.'

We step outside into the fresh air and laugh together. The ice is well and truly broken.

Elizabeth looks across at me. 'I wanted to contact you earlier, to say we could meet somewhere else, before James arrived. Maybe in the Mont Clare hotel across the road. Then I realised I didn't have your number.'

We walk slowly towards Nassau Street. I notice we are the same height, shoulder to shoulder.

'Let's go somewhere quiet. You know Dublin better than me.' Elizabeth places her hand on my shoulder and I feel a sudden surge of affection for her. It is like the roles are reversed now. I am being looked after, not by a daughter, but someone very close, almost like a sister. We make our way up Grafton Street among the Saturday shoppers and turn into the little street leading to The Westbury.

'It's always quiet here.'

We find a corner, over by a window, with plush green armchairs. We sit side by side, a low table in front of us, looking out onto a side street. This time I order, and ask Elizabeth if she'd like something to eat. But we are both too preoccupied to really think of our appetites.

'Tell me about yourself.'

Elizabeth laughs. 'I've told you most of the main details in that long letter. The only thing that has changed is that I've finished with my boyfriend. And I've at last met you.' She reaches towards me and holds my hand. She holds it for what seems like a long time.

I open my handbag and reach into it. 'I have something here for you.' I pass her the bulky gift box.

Elizabeth opens the present I have brought, then looks down at the door knocker in the shape of a Claddagh ring, one heart held by two hands.

'Just in case you don't want to meet me again.'

She looks at me as if I've said something shocking. 'We've only just met and you're thinking of abandoning me again?'

'I didn't mean it that way, Elizabeth! The door knocker means you can call on me anytime. That I will always be here for you.' I trail off into a stream of babbling words, thinking how silly my present is, and how foolish my words.

A pang of guilt runs through me, and I'm ashamed of my artless ramblings. I wasn't there for her for the past twenty-six years but she is here now for me. It is she who is the brave soul, the one showing maternal compassion. That deep chasm may still be there, but the air between us is humming with possibilities.

I know all is not lost when Elizabeth breaks into a big smile.

'It's beautiful! Of course I'll want to see you again.'

The waitress brings our tea and again Elizabeth takes control. 'I won't say "let me be mother".' Her blue eyes light up again. They are a very definite shade of blue. Another one of the mysteries of genetics, because both Brian and myself have hazel eyes.

'Isn't it a coincidence that we are both teachers?' She tells me about her university job, where she lectures in the women's studies department.

'I will be in Dublin again soon, Phyl. Can we meet then?'

This is not the end, I tell myself. It is only the beginning of the beginning. I listen carefully to the soft ebb and flow of her voice as she tells me about her brother's children. Her voice is nothing like mine or Brian's. A few months later, when I meet her parents, I discover that she speaks exactly like her mother.

Our next meeting is in the Gresham Hotel. Elizabeth has spent the day at a women's studies conference in UCD. She is elated at meeting so many academics and listening to so many papers from so many Irish and UK universities. We find a quiet corner in the lounge and order our drinks.

'So good to see you.' She reaches out, takes my hand and holds it tightly. 'I've been thinking about you so much.'

The drinks arrive, two glasses of Heineken. We clink our glasses. I notice now that when she smiles, the contours of her face dimple in exactly the same way as Brian's. I am bursting with love for this beautiful intelligent girl sitting beside me.

'It's like I've found that piece of the puzzle I'd lost. And now, here you are!' Elizabeth beams at me.

'I can say the very same thing,' I say. 'I feel exactly the same.' Her openness delights me, and the sound of her voice enchants me. I am hypnotised by her very presence. 'How was your conference, Elizabeth?'

'Superb. It's fascinating to hear of other people's research papers.'

'Are you engaged in any areas of research?' I'm curious to know what her interests are in the area of women's studies.

'Yes, actually: nature and nurture. I have many friends who are adopted.' Elizabeth tells me later that when she started school two of her best friends were adopted, so she thought then that everyone was.

We are on our third glass of Heineken when she puts down her glass and, in a serious voice, says, 'Phyl, you were robbed.'

I am puzzled. I don't know how to respond. I can't follow her line of thought at all. The sudden switching of tracks.

Then Elizabeth says, 'Why didn't you keep me?'

This is a huge question. Probably *the question,* in fact. I should have known was going to come up. I should have prepared a proper answer. I am guilty of presuming she knows all the answers. That she understands that for me to keep and rear her at that time would have brought shame on the family. It would have made both of us outcasts in the society that existed then.

I want to say that it is something I will explain at a later stage. That I know it isn't a trick question and that she needs a serious answer. She has already told me that during her university studies she has written essays on why young girls handed up their children for adoption. She quotes some of those facts now.

In 1967 (the year of her adoption) 97 per cent of babies born to unmarried women in Ireland were handed up for adoption. She is included in this stark statistic. That the other three per cent of women who kept their babies would have been people from either wealthy families or those who could rise above the social mores and prejudice of the time.

What she is really asking me, of course, is not why I had abandoned her, as a general sociological sort of question, but how I, personally, could have done such a thing. No, this isn't an academic question at all; this is a question from a real person—my own daughter.

I think carefully before speaking. A few misspoken words could do a lot of damage now.

I begin: 'It was only weeks after I left St Patrick's that the reality of what I had done came crashing down on me, Elizabeth.' I pause a moment to let that sink in. Then I continue slowly. 'I rang up the convent and asked for my baby. I told them I wanted you back. The nun on the phone let me ramble on a bit. Then she said, calmly and clearly, that if I didn't stop whinging, she would leave you on my mother's doorstep the following morning.'

'I understand. I do. I really do,' Elizabeth says, but somehow I feel, deep down, that she doesn't really. That the words don't connect with her. Don't convince her, emotionally anyway.

A distance has clearly been created between us now, after my feeble, fumbled explanation. Still, I feel I owe her a further explanation. At a later stage I will try to tell her the truth: that there would have been no room for her in my family home. Not only because it was an overcrowded house, but because she would have been exposed to the hostile social, political and religious environment that existed at the time.

Nor do I tell her that I gazed into the face of every little girl I saw for years after parting with her, to see if I could find some resemblance to her. That I was like a detective looking for clues in every family setting that was new to me.

In silence, we take a taxi together, outside the hotel. Elizabeth is staying with her brother, who lives not too far from my own rented accommodation. She tells me later that when she was getting out of the taxi, the driver asked her if she and her girlfriend had a good night on the town. She replied that this was no girlfriend but her own mother. The taxi man too fell silent.

A few weeks later Elizabeth asks me to meet her mother. We are to meet in the Shelbourne Hotel on Stephen's Green. My head is crammed with conflicting questions now. Will this be a woman-to-woman meeting? Or more a mother-to-mother meeting? Should I say thank you for minding my baby? But no, that would be insulting to the woman who is now Elizabeth's mother. To the woman who has nurtured and loved her and accepted her as her own daughter. Anyway, the simple truth is, she knows Elizabeth better than me, better than I ever could. Again Elizabeth was the one who looked after us both as we chatted and I really can't remember what the conversation was about because I was so nervous.

Looking back now I realise that Elizabeth was the adult at this meeting. She was the one who mothered both of us at this time, the meeting of her two mothers.

With the passage of time, I meet Elizabeth's father, her sister and brother. I can see clearly that her family love her. At one stage Elizabeth's mother tells me that when she was young, they would say a prayer for me every night when saying the family rosary.

It isn't only her family I meet in that first year of our reunion. Elizabeth is very open about her whole world. When I visit Galway, she introduces me to her friends as her mother. I am in heaven then, and feel we are definitely in love with each other.

24. PARIS DAYS

I hear a young woman's voice in the distance, outside my door. She is chatting in fluent, flawless French to the concierge. I suddenly recognise the voice. It is coming closer. And now there is a knock. I open the door slowly to Elizabeth. I can just about see the top of her head behind a huge bouquet of red roses.

'For you, Phyl.'

I bury my face in the roses, inhaling not only the scent but the essence of her beautiful presence. This is not the first time Elizabeth has presented me with flowers. She met me a few months earlier at Cork railway station with a bunch of yellow freesias. 'They're beautiful...really beautiful.'

'Just like you,' she says. She has a way of always making me feel good about myself. 'How was your flight?' Before I can draw breath she says, 'I've booked a table in the Latin Quarter for seven o'clock.'

Elizabeth has invited me to Paris for a few days during her summer holidays. She has been invited to present a paper at the Sorbonne. It is near the Centre Culturel Irlandais, where she has arranged accommodation for me. Since her student days she has been a frequent visitor to France. Her professional exchange programmes and friendships over the years have made her almost one of the locals.

We walk to the restaurant in high spirits. I feel like a young girl going on an adventure with my new best friend. The cocktail of scents on this June evening are intoxicating. The scent of Elizabeth's red roses and the bougainvillea vines on the walls makes me giddy. I know that I am in Paris now. I have arrived at an altogether new place on the map and in my life.

When we turn a corner, it is as if we have entered another sort of world. The streets become narrower. People are eating at tables along the street, chatting animatedly. It looks like a detail from the Degas print I have on my living room wall. The euphonic burble of French accents wafts through the air as we pass restaurant after restaurant.

'This one is ours.' The head waiter knows Elizabeth and he kisses her on both cheeks. Then she introduces me: 'Ma mère.'

I am suddenly undone again and feel wrong-footed. I feel like an imposter, while at the same time enjoying this role. I am happy in a way that I've never experienced before in my life. Now, I am somebody. Not only am I in Paris with my beautiful girl, but I'm being introduced as her mother.

'The specials tonight are prawns,' Elizabeth says with a smile. I know exactly why she is amused. Our first meal together, in Dublin, was in a restaurant beside the Project Arts Centre. I suggested we meet there for lunch as it was the 'in' place to go. I ordered the prawns, but when they arrived at the table all I could see was a family of beady black eyes looking up at me through coats of glistening gold.

'This is how to eat them,' Elizabeth said then, as she deftly pulled each section apart. She did it in such a way that I didn't feel embarrassed by my lack of culinary etiquette.

'No, not again!'

Elizabeth laughed. 'There are easier options, you know.' She reads out the menu and translates. When she reads out 'Boeuf Bourguignon' I know I'm in safe territory.

The waiter takes our order and I realise that I'm ravenous. I haven't eaten since leaving Dublin Airport that morning.

When we have eaten Elizabeth looks across the table at me. 'You must be tired, Phyl?'

I am a little tired but I'm not thinking of bed just yet. I feel like stretching my legs and taking in a little more of our immediate area. I am in Paris, after all.

Elizabeth smiles over at me. 'We could make the Luxembourg Gardens before the gates close.'

'That sounds good.'

'I can show you the Sorbonne and the place beside it where I'm staying during the conference.' Elizabeth is the Irish representative and will read her paper in French. 'There are representatives from all over Europe at this conference,' she explains. 'I'm really looking forward to hearing their papers.'

That's my girl, I think to myself. A huge wave of admiration for her comes over me, knowing now that she carries her accolades so lightly. I think back, a little ruefully, to what my niece Katherine said when I first told her about Elizabeth's achievements. 'You can't take any credit for that, Phyl. You didn't bring her up.'

No, I didn't bring her up. That much is true, of course. She has her own parents. But she is my flesh and blood and that must mean something, mustn't it? No human being has any claim on another, all of that I know, but there has to be some connection between blood relatives. But then again siblings can be so different to each other, even though they all entered the world from the same womb. All I know is that at this moment I feel so close to her and I want this time to go on forever.

We walk towards the traffic lights opposite the Luxembourg Gardens. Elizabeth slips her arm through mine. Then she starts to hum the Edith Piaf song, *Non, je ne regrette rien*. It has been playing on a loop in the restaurant during our meal.

'No regrets,' she whispers. We walk across the road and in through the big gates.

'I love this place,' Elizabeth says, as we walk towards the wide-open space. We pass a group of middle-aged men and women engaged in graceful Tai Chi movements. 'You could give a yoga class here,' she says.

I smile at her.

'I'm not joking, Phyl. You're a qualified teacher now.'

I had recently qualified as a yoga teacher in Cork. When I was being assessed by my supervisor for the final class, Elizabeth had kindly brought a group of her students to take part during one of her visits to Cork university. She stops all of a sudden, stretching her arms up to the sky and performs the first sequences of Salute to the Sun with utter grace of movement.

'Wonderful.' I say, 'I feel at home here.' I link my arm into hers.

A flutter of mini-sail boats catch my eye in the distance, reminding me of swans sailing on the surface of a lake.

'Aren't they like children playing with their toys.'

'Yes, French people know how to play, and most of all they know how to be happy.'

Of course, this is where my parents thought I was when I was in hiding my secret, the one that is in the open now and is the girl walking by my side.

The light of the day is beginning to fade slowly.

'I'll walk you back to the centre, Phyl.' At the gate to the Centre Culturel, Elizabeth embraces me and whispers in my ear, *'Dors avec les anges.'*

Even my school French can translate that much. There and then, I decide that Elizabeth is my angel. Her generosity and warmth are so impressive, and I feel blessed.

Sleep does not come easily. I am in strange waters now, one way or the other, with a young woman I am only slowly getting to know. A young woman who charms and excites me and impresses me so much. A woman I want to know every single thing about. I am in love. There is no other way I can express it. This must surely be the state of grace that mothers feel, I tell myself—mothers who are blessed with children they have reared from birth. The umbilical cord is never completely severed, and I'm again reminded of the many incidents when my physical body remembered or was triggered by incidents that took me right back to my closeness to my baby girl. The body remembers, but I was guilty of not listening to the messages. I am acutely conscious now of the time I have to make up. The lost time.

After a while, I settle down and, just as Elizabeth wished for me, I sleep with the angels.

At 10am we get off the metro at Rue du Bac. We walk down a side street until we come to a big church—the Chapel of Our Lady of the Miraculous Medal—mother house of the Daughters of Charity, I read from the glass encased noticeboard outside the church, and the place where the Virgin Mary appeared to Saint Catherine Laboure in 1830, asking her to create a medal later known as the Miraculous Medal.

We walk into the church together. 'Miracles have happened here on this site.' Elizabeth holds my hand and leads me to a seat. 'I want to tell you something now that I heard a few years ago, Phyl.'

I look into her face like a child waiting to be told a fairytale. She closes her eyes and says, 'Let's think, for a moment, about the good nuns that looked after your letters here.'

I don't really get where this is going. The nuns at St Patrick's were always good to me, to tell the truth, but I have no idea what Elizabeth is going to say next.

'The nun who sent your letters here was my aunt. My Auntie Síle, as we called her.'

But how could that be? I am desperately trying to make sense of this now. How could a nun who was in St Patrick's when I was there be Elizabeth's aunt—and not related to me? Surely one of those nuns would have told me if we were related? I was thinking backwards. This was the reason Elizabeth had brought me to this church. But it was like looking at a jigsaw without the accompanying picture to guide me.

'Auntie Síle, that nun, was my mother's sister.'

Now it is clear. Elizabeth's other mother. The mother who adopted her and brought her up.

'And is she here in this convent? I'd love to meet her.'

‘No, she died many years ago. But she did retire here before her death.’

‘What was she like?’ I ask, because I don’t remember the names of any of the nuns, except for the Mother Superior, Sister Joseph, and Sister Lawrence.

‘Unfortunately, I never met her. She died when I was a child.’

‘So your Aunt Síle would have known me during my time in St Pat’s? In the mother and baby home?’

Elizabeth takes my hand in hers and kisses me on the cheek. ‘She would have known me too, remember! I was there also.’

‘Of course. She would have, you were such an adorable baby.’

We walk around the church and I spot, at the top altar, figures of angels playing harps and flutes. For a moment I feel I am in some sort of paradise. We light candles at every altar for this nun. It feels as if we are performing a sort of benediction to the memory of Sister Síle. On our way out, we visit the shop at the side of the church and buy a collection of large miraculous medals.

We saunter down Rue du Bac and stop at a corner cafe. Elizabeth greets the man behind the counter and we sit down by the window. A warm glow floods through my veins. I feel a strange new affection now for this nun who chose me and my baby for her own sister. A person who thought that I had given birth to a baby worthy of her own family connections.

It would be a long time before Aunt Síle was mentioned again. By then, I would have come to the conclusion that she must have been the nun who opened and read my letters to my parents before sending them on to Paris. That she would have known quite a lot about me. That she had chosen my baby girl for her sister.

It took many years for me to parse the generally good treatment I had in St Pat’s, leaving aside the actual day of Elizabeth’s birth. Was it because this nun, Elizabeth’s mother’s sister, had chosen me as a special case? Perhaps. And was she the nun who organised the French dress for my homecoming? I would never know.

It is my last night in Paris. Elizabeth has booked a Greek restaurant in another part of the city. Before dinner, we amble through the streets. My heart lifts again at all the gaiety in the air. At the sight of people of all ages holding hands. French people certainly know how to show affection, unlike us Irish. The colourful displays in shop windows and outside as we walk along are uplifting, dazzling displays with multicoloured blossoms covering the paths like patchwork quilts. Next door to one flower shop, I spot a scarf boutique, with great swatches of silk draped around the walls like sails on a boat. I ask Elizabeth to choose one for herself. Then I buy one for myself too, so that I can carry this experience home with me.

The restaurant brings me back to one of my first holidays. It was in Greece during my time working in Aer Lingus, in the 1960s. We took a plane to Athens and a boat to Mykonos Island. No holiday since has matched the magic of what my untravelled 18-year-old self-experienced then. And here I am now, in the company of a much-travelled 26-year-old young woman.

After the meal the music starts. There are few people in the restaurant, so our table receives a lot of attention from the dancer. Images of broken plates and stamping feet come back to me when a man approaches and, without a word, hoists Elizabeth onto an empty table. He claps his hands in time as she shuffles her feet and moves her hips to the music with unembarrassed abandon. That's my girl, I think again.

On the way back to the centre, Elizabeth tells me that she is a frequent visitor to the Greek restaurant. The dancer knows her and her friends, who always join in the dancing. She will be spending time with these friends after the conference at the Sorbonne. She feels at home in Paris. How different our time in Paris would be if had I followed my dream of going to Paris as an au pair after leaving Sandymount High School. Of course, my parents wouldn't allow me to travel at that age. And anyway, even if they had, I wouldn't now be here with Elizabeth. *C'est la vie...*

We part outside the gate of the centre. Elizabeth puts her arms around me and we cling to each other for a long time. 'I hate goodbyes, Phyl!'

'I do too.'

I look at her beautiful face and see she that she is a little tired. It has been a long day for her too, I remind myself. 'Good luck with your paper tomorrow.'

She shrugs her shoulders. 'I wish it wasn't an early morning one. Anyway, *bon voyage,* and please text me when you arrive home.'

And then she is gone. My lovely daughter. My only child.

25. MEETING MY MOTHER

I grew closer to my mother on the heels of my reunion with Elizabeth. I began to see her in a new light, understanding the hardships she had endured when rearing her family. I took to visiting every Sunday. Our routine was simple. I finally had my mother to myself. After lunch, we would go out walking to a nearby park, or sometimes to Mount Jerome cemetery to visit my father's grave.

My mother was a great gardener and loved looking at the floral arrangements as we strolled around all the different areas of the cemetery. Graveyards can be enchanting places, once the pain of loss has eased. She pointed out the flowers. 'They're like table settings. You have to be careful how you choose and arrange your plants.'

My life went on through its changes. I was in my early fifties when I passed my driving test. Our Sunday afternoons changed direction altogether then. Now we had wheels. The first adventure was to Bray, not too far because of my lack of driving experience. My mother proved the most relaxed passenger and never once commented on my driving faults.

'I always dreamed that I would live near the sea, in a house in Wicklow,' she said on our first outing. She was a countrywoman to her very bones and never felt at home in Dublin. She never liked the poky house where she reared eleven children with an eternal struggle to keep food on the table.

How could you live in a house that you didn't like? The answer is quite simple: money. My father didn't earn enough for a bigger house. But lack of money didn't prevent the making of a bigger family.

'I promise to take you to every little seaside place in Wicklow,' I told her one day as I struggled to find the right gear going uphill in Greystones. On these outings we would always find a hotel and relax with afternoon tea. That Sunday, as we sat looking out at the sea and chatting about this and that, I realised that, for the first time my mother was beginning to open up and talk to me about her feelings. I think that she was reflecting on a life lived as it neared its end.

Feelings, desires, particularly those of women, were rarely heard back then. There was no vocabulary. Nobody asked a woman, 'What do you want, What do you desire.' Women's' voices were silent.

The following year she was about to turn ninety. My mother didn't look anything like an old woman. Her skin was smooth and wrinkle-free and her mobility was every bit as good as mine.

'If I could wave a magic wand and wish you anything in the world for your birthday, what would you wish for?' My eyes fixed on hers.

She thought for a moment before answering. 'To be ten years younger,' she said, without hesitation. That wasn't the answer I had been expecting. But what a present that would be, if we could only go backwards with each birthday. Go backwards and perhaps correct our mistakes. Or better still, satisfy our real desires. If only I were ten years younger, perhaps I could become pregnant again?

My mother looked out at the white sails floating by in the distance. Then she turned to look over at me with an expression in her eyes that I wasn't familiar with. It was almost as if she were seeing me for the very first time.

'Isn't it time I met your daughter, Phyl?' Her voice was tender and touching, and her timing was just right.

Although it may seem strange now, it had never occurred to me up to that point that any member of the family would want to meet my daughter. A cloud of silence had descended on my siblings when the news was first revealed. It was an uncomfortable silence—nobody's fault, really, just an inability to find the right words, as always. It had never occurred to me either, that Elizabeth might want to meet any of my siblings. She had, in fact, bumped into one of my sisters with her husband and daughter when she visited my house unexpectedly one day. On another such visit, she had met my nephew and his family.

My mother's request shook me. It disturbed me, and I wasn't sure why. At the time, I couldn't decode my confused response. Was I trying to protect Elizabeth and keep her all to myself? Or was it more that I didn't trust my own family?

Though my mother's request came as a bombshell, I knew I had to honour her wishes. Elizabeth herself, as it happened, was very open to meeting her new grandmother, and so date and location were settled. All that was left was to organise bringing my mother to the Orwell Lodge in Rathgar, a hotel she was already familiar with.

It was arranged that my sister Mary would drive my mother to the hotel and then let my mother enter ahead of her, so that she could be with her daughter and granddaughter. My sister would reappear after a decent interval and meet her niece. Elizabeth would come to my house beforehand and we would both walk to the hotel to be there before my mother's arrival.

When Elizabeth arrived at my house that day, she was carrying a beautiful bunch of blue irises. I was astonished. 'How did you know they were one of my mother's favourite flowers?' Elizabeth smiled but said nothing. My beautiful daughter always surprised me, but the flowers blew my mind.

'I've got butterflies in my tummy,' she confessed.

'Everything will be fine,' I reassured her. 'What can go wrong?'

In a lifetime of knowing my mother, I had never witnessed her being so at ease with another person. I was transfixed by the exchange that took place. Her face lit up when Elizabeth offered her the flowers. When tea was brought to us, Elizabeth took charge, pouring tea for my mother and me, and asking my mother if she took sugar.

'I hope your family are well,' my mother offered. Her next words were about me. 'You've made my daughter very happy.' She looked at me with tears in her eyes. 'So, tell me about your life, Elizabeth.'

It was clear that my dear mother had given the meeting deep thought in advance. She spoke with such a graceful ease and wise insight. As I watched these two women engage with each other—the two people I cherished most in the world—I noticed the marked similarity in their profiles as they drew closer. I could sense the unfolding of generations now, like my multicoloured Russian dolls, each one contained in the other, each separate yet flowing into the other.

My sister arrived to the hotel at the agreed time to greet Elizabeth and to take my mother home. When we left the hotel, I took a photo of my mother holding the irises, with Elizabeth by her side. I was so proud of both of them, and happy for them.

26. A FUNERAL

1999

It all seemed a bit unreal, standing together at the graveside where my mother was about to be buried. A place we had strolled to on many a Sunday afternoon, taking in the styles of headstones and settings. Now, she herself would be part of one of the plots she had described as table-tops to be decorated tastefully.

I would make sure to look after her grave—a promise made to her on one of our Mount Jerome walks: I would be her grave-keeper, the keeper of the flame. It was half in banter then, but now it was real. My mind was struggling with other matters at the same time. My long-lost baby girl was standing among my family, among the tribe she was physically part of and yet separated from. Hardly anyone spoke to her. This was not the day for me to be critical of my siblings. After all, they too were grieving the loss of our mother. But I couldn't help noticing how few acknowledged her presence, or so I thought at the time.

As we were coming out of the church I spotted my nephew Garret, around the same age as Elizabeth, locking eyes with her. They held that connection for a moment and I wondered afterwards whether it wasn't a moment of spontaneous attraction.

There is something that happens to the mind in moments of grief. It's as if you have been catapulted into a state where the film of your life is played out right in front of you. You become a spectator, watching and waiting to see what might happen next.

I was aware that I was gripping the medal of Our Lady tightly in the palm of my hand, the one from the church in Rue du Bac, thinking back to the lovely time I had enjoyed in Paris with Elizabeth. Would she be standing here at my graveside in a few years? Would she be grieving the loss of a mother—this mother, me?

I reminded myself that I had only known her for six of her thirty-two years. Was it possible to make up for lost time? Her real mother was aware of where she was at this moment—at the funeral of her birth mother's mother. And that woman had known her daughter since she was six weeks old, had nurtured and cared for her.

A few days before the funeral, I had read the Seamus Heaney poem *When All the Others were Away at Mass* to Elizabeth. A poem that resonated with me. The young Seamus Heaney is peeling potatoes beside his mother when all his siblings are away at mass. A common enough practice in our house when we were children. Each time I came to the line *Never closer the whole rest of our lives,* my voice broke. 'If that happens at the funeral, I'll be by your side,' Elizabeth had assured me. And here she was now, by my side at the graveside. And in the church earlier, right beside me, and when the funeral cortège had walked behind my mother's coffin up the avenue to Mount Argus church.

Elizabeth's name had been made public in my mother's death notices in the newspapers, as one of my mother's grandchildren. Yet, here we were, all together at the graveside of my mother—and yet still apart. What did Elizabeth think when she saw my seven brothers and three sisters sitting in the front row of the church? Did she say to herself, are these my aunts and uncles? Did she feel part of the ribbon of genes running down the generations?

The medal of Our Lady was still in my hand, and I held it tighter now, feeling the presence of Elizabeth at my side. Knowing that meeting her was the best day of my life and losing my mother the worst. Making a move towards the grave, I lowered the medal on top of my mother's coffin. I'm not sure why I did this, but I think that it was the hope that the coming together of mothers might somehow strengthen the love-bond between this mother and this child. I prayed to my mother to let this happen, to please let me bond again with my girl.

After the burial we moved across the road to a local pub. My mother's wishes for her funeral had been well known to us, most importantly her wish that a hot meal be served to everyone. She was, of course, thinking of all her relatives from Wexford who would have travelled up to Dublin for the funeral. Above all, she wanted us to continue together as a family. As the meal was being served, I looked around the room at the different tables, at my blood relatives spread out like a deck of cards, and wondered what Elizabeth thought of them. I recalled something someone once said about playing with the cards you were dealt at birth. He said you could always change those cards. How could I?

After the meal we retired to the family home. As we entered the house, my younger sister Eileen looked at Elizabeth and said, 'I feel I should carry you across the threshold!' Elizabeth's anxious face broke into a broad smile. Later my brother Noel surprised me when he said, 'I watched her as she fixed your scarf when we were leaving the pub. Jesus, that was love.' It surprised me that he would say it to me, but I know that the situation must have been hard for everyone. Elizabeth had now met my siblings, been part of my mother's funeral and visited the house where I was reared. I thought now that Elizabeth must surely know everything about me that she needed to know.

Years later, Elizabeth told me that she was very moved at my mother's funeral when one of my brothers lifted her into the air when he met her first. But I had missed that gesture.

Over the weeks to the cusp of the year 2000, a Millennium Candle was delivered to every household in Ireland to mark the new century. The idea was to bid farewell to the millennium as a nation, and to welcome in the new one. On New Year's Eve, Elizabeth called to my house to ring in the New Year with me.

We watched Joe Dolan sing his heart out on RTÉ, the sweat rolling down his face as he sang, 'It's You, It's You, It's You.' Then we lit the Millennium Candle and clinked our glasses and said, 'Here's to many more New Years together!' I took a photo of Elizabeth sitting at the table beside the candle and Christmas tree, little knowing that it would be her last New Year's Eve sitting at my table. Every household in the country was also given details of a specially planted tree and told the exact location of that tree. I knew then that the tree that my mother told me resided inside myself would be showing marks of a change in my relationship with Elizabeth.

The following year, to mark the first anniversary of my mother's death, Elizabeth invited me on another holiday to France. We would spend Christmas Day together in Grenoble, but we would start with a night in Paris. That first night was in the Esmeralda hotel, near Notre Dame Cathedral, around the corner from the Shakespeare and Company bookshop. It marked the first time we had shared a bedroom together. I was about to pull the duvet around me and settle down to sleep when I saw Elizabeth get out of bed to turn off the light. She looked like a little schoolgirl in her pink attire.

'I love those pyjamas,' I said.

'They're one of Mum's Christmas presents. She said they would keep me warm and cosy when I was away with you.'

The expression on my face must have changed, it was an emotion that rose up unbidden.

'Phyl, you're my mother, but Nora, is my Mum.'

Although, I knew all of this, my unbridled envy and regret shocked me. Whatever it was, I knew my place now. I wasn't Elizabeth's Mum and I had no right to expect anything from her.

It struck me some time later that all my important relationships were shared ones—shared with a third party. It's not strictly true, of course, that I shared Brian with his wife, though there is a grain of truth in it. I had lived with Brendan for nearly twenty years knowing his heart was with another woman. And now my one and only child had to be shared with another mother. It took a lot more time, though, for me to accept that all of these relationships were ones of my own devising.

27. THE BEGINNING OF THE END

It started quietly at first. Elizabeth was in Dublin visiting friends when she called into me. As always, I was delighted to see her. She placed a fancy packet on the kitchen table. 'This is from the new tea-shop on Wicklow Street.'

I watched her as she tidied away the newspapers from the table, setting a space for our tea ritual, and putting on the kettle. It was wonderful to see how she made herself at home now.

'It's new. China tea with pear.'

I was a Barry's Tea woman myself and was beginning to explore other brands like Earl Grey, but I would try anything that Elizabeth recommended.

'It's almost intoxicating.' There was a slight change in her tone of voice as she poured the tea and I sensed right away that something was out of kilter.

'It's finished, over.'

'What's finished? What's over?' For one terrible moment, I thought she was talking about us.

Elizabeth had discussed all her relationships with me and had always encouraged me to do the same. I had met the man she was talking about. I knew him to be a loving and decent person. 'He's going abroad. It's the end. It's the end of everything.'

I wanted to put my arms around her now. I had known all about heartbreak myself—of being in love with a man who was not available. What words are there to console a young woman whose heart has been shattered?

'You know all about it, don't you?' She looked at me in a beseeching way. All I could say was that I did.

'There are other men who adore you.' She had many male admirers in her life. But it was the wrong thing to say.

Elizabeth bridled. 'You really shouldn't have said that, Phyl.' Her normally calm voice was now angry.

I couldn't unsay what I had said. But I had to try.

'I'm sorry,' I said slowly.

'I don't want to hear any more of your clichés!'

As she was leaving, I tried to embrace her, but she was suddenly beyond my reach. A shadow had been cast over our afternoon.

A few weeks passed before we spoke again, and this time it was on the phone. I was so glad to hear her voice. But the tone wasn't friendly. What had I done to cause this change in her behaviour?

She had been lost to me for many years, then miraculously found. I couldn't bear to lose her again. Up until now, I'd had the pleasure of her closeness and friendship, and, most important of all, her love. My house was full of cards and notes written to me telling me how much she loved me and how wonderful I was. My whole world had been renewed, enriched by her very existence. She had said many times, 'No matter what happens, Phyl, I'll always be on your side.'

It was weeks later when Elizabeth wrote to me to say she was going through a bad time and trying to recover from her break-up. That she wouldn't be in touch for a while.

Was this her way of telling me that our relationship was over? I walked around my home looking at all the reminders of her presence in my life: the baby photograph sent to me by the nuns, her photo sent to me when we first exchanged letters before our first meeting and the one celebrating our tenth anniversary—ten wonderful years. Where had everything gone wrong? Why couldn't we talk about it? Hadn't we always said that if one of us offended the other we would verbalise our feelings? Or had I imagined that?

I gazed at other photo memories, including ones of our happy time in Paris, and the last photo taken of her sitting by the Millennium Candle. My kitchen fridge was festooned with magnets, and there were mugs, cups and saucers, all presented to me by Elizabeth. I didn't know how to deal with being punished for those actions Elizabeth perceived me to have carried out.

But neither could I fully understand the nature of her wounds in relation to being abandoned at birth. That was the real truth. I had thought that we had discussed everything and clarified everything. Looking back now, though, I realise that I really had presumed, yet again, that she had understood our story. But I was wrong. I had been guilty of assuming too much.

I had treated Elizabeth as a close friend and a sister. Not like a daughter at all. The role of mother was new to me, I didn't know how to behave. I cannot speak for how Elizabeth felt at this time, but it did seem to me that she had become critical of me; it was almost like the way a teenager can turn against a parent, but she wasn't a teenager and I really wasn't a parent, not a proper one anyway. I was a woman with flaws, and far from perfect.

Life continued. I had recently been promoted to head of the drama department in Liberties College and had been given extra responsibilities. As well as teaching, I had to produce reports and attend meetings. I was beginning to feel the strain. The cause of the strain, though, wasn't my job because I loved my place of work. It was as if I was feeling that huge absence again.

The terror of losing my child for the second time was altogether unbearable. A friend of mine suggested that I visit a psychotherapist. She pointed out that I had never really processed the experience of being pregnant and then losing my baby to adoption. I hadn't dealt with the sad reality of living for twenty-six years with this secret inside me. Eventually I gave in and went to see the therapist she recommended.

I had never been to therapy before and was of the opinion that it was only for hopeless cases. The therapist's office was in a leafy district in Dublin 4, not far from where I lived. As I walked to my first visit, I pondered how I would start the session, or indeed, how the therapist would start it. When I got to her office, I was pleasantly surprised to find a room full of light with plants and colourful paintings and comfortable chairs.

Jacquie, was a small woman with a kind face, curly fair hair and a broad smile. I liked her immediately. Her voice was low and clear and she reminded me of a kind teacher I had a crush on in Sandymount High. After a few moments of silence when I was slowly consumed by terror she said, 'Just think of yourself riding a bicycle downhill, and then stop wherever you want to.'

My first words to her were, 'I don't know where to begin.' There was a pause, and then I started thinking about my bicycle going downhill and of the blue bicycle my father bought me during my Sandymount High days. All I could see now was the face of Elizabeth. That was where I would begin. I went back to how I had met Brian and how our relationship had begun. I told Jacquie about our first intimate connection, when I sat on his knee in a bedsit after the last night of *The Highest House on the Mountain* more than thirty-six years before.

From her perspective, Brian's actions were clearly abusive. She spoke then of the lack of consent, a word that wasn't charged with the same meaning it has today. Those were different times, a different climate, a different country, I tried to tell myself.

'Did he force himself on you, Phyl?' Jacquie said forthrightly. She was opening my eyes to the fact that Brian's behaviour could well be deemed completely unacceptable.

I had to be honest with her. He had, in a certain way, forced himself on me. True, I had wanted to be close to him, but not in the way that it happened.

I was still free-wheeling down that hill, flying against the wind. Admitting to myself now that he was the only man in my life that I really desired. So much so that I hadn't even allowed myself to consider his wife or children. I had been living in a fantasy fairytale for years.

Jacquie ended the session by saying simply, 'Brian was the first man you fell in love with, and you became pregnant after your first time of having sex. Yes?'

I thought of all the lost years I had squandered. Elizabeth was the one good thing from those years. She was the only good result of that life. She was the fruit of my life.

We explored my other relationships over the years. I had met many truly good men who didn't attract me. Jacquie pointed out that the men who did attract me were men who were not emotionally available. It seemed there was a pattern here: all the people I had fallen in love with were really in love with someone else. And now the person I really loved and wanted to love me was also in love with someone else—another mother, who was not me either. Her final question made me really have a good look at myself: Is there something in your behaviour that attracts these men, something you do to enable such relationships?

Walking home that evening, I felt a lot lighter. The trees were showing the first signs of new life, tight little green buds about to burst open. I thought of the Monet exhibition I had seen in Paris with Elizabeth, where the room was filled with an abundance of budding trees bathed in light. Was it possible that the human spirit could be reborn again with new life? I felt hopeful that all would be well.

For the first time in months, my anxiety lifted, even though there was still no communication from Elizabeth. I continued my weekly visits to Jacquie for the next few weeks.

It was true. I had accepted bad behaviour from men I was attracted to, and was bored by men who were 'nice.' I didn't give these men much of a chance. That was another learning curve for me. I felt now that it would probably take me another fifty years to get it right.

'But you haven't wasted your life. Look at all you have achieved!' Jacquie reminded me that I had had a successful career as a teacher and had discovered my own creativity through theatre and writing. Above all, she said, you have developed your own agency in the world. Your world. 'At some stage of our lives, we have to give birth to ourselves. It's not roots we are concerned about but being rooted.' I had to ask myself was I ever rooted?

These words were so true, I had lived these words, and I couldn't undo the past. But for the moment, there was no word from Elizabeth. The silence was beginning to worry me more and more. I felt now that I had to do something. Elizabeth needed time to recover from her own heartbreak, and I felt helpless at not being able to console her. To telephone would have been intrusive. A good friend I had confided in advised me to write to her. This friend is the most articulate person I know. And at this time, I was lost for words. In fact, I was completely frozen emotionally and incapable of any action.

Lara was a woman who had been meditating since the time I first knew her, back in our university days. She had a deep belief in the liminal energy between the worlds of the living and the dead. Her mother had recently died, and Lara still felt a strong connection with her during her meditations. One day, she came to me and said that her mother had dictated a letter to her for Elizabeth.

I was bowled over by this, as if it was a sign from heaven. I took the whole letter as gospel, in fact, and sent it to Elizabeth. These were not my words but I believed them to be inspired words and beyond my own ability. The theme of the letter was 'We are all here on this planet to learn from our life's journey, and our task is to work through the challenges so that we can evolve.' My thinking was not agile enough to know that sending this was entirely ill-advised. The reality was, I felt a terrible sense of panic that I had to communicate in some way, as I believed that otherwise I would lose my Elizabeth forever.

But this letter backfired hugely. Elizabeth was deeply offended by it. 'It was cruel,' she said, when she finally phoned. She added, 'I showed it to my friends and they agreed with me.' At a later stage she said that the letter was one of rejection; she said she wasn't affected by my first rejection but by the second rejection, the one contained in this letter.

Looking back now, I see how desperate I was to mend the breach. I should never have sent that letter. I should have just told her that I would always be there for her. I should have stood back, however hard it was for me.

On my next visit to Jacquie, I discussed the letter. 'You are an articulate woman, Phyl. Why didn't you trust your own words?' I had to face up to the fact that I had lost confidence in myself. Elizabeth, too, had become so very critical of me, and I didn't trust myself to be coherent when dealing with her.

At the end of the session, Jacquie said, 'Research studies into the reunification of mothers and children show that it is a common feature for the child in adulthood to reverse the act of abandonment and reject the birth parent.'

I walked home feeling the terrible chill that these words sent through me. Was I being abandoned now? Was it my turn to suffer that terrible fate?

Jacquie had said in a previous session that some events in life are so timelessly wounding that few people escape the arrows of hurt, and that our life lesson was to learn to live with these hurts. I decided to take all of her wise words on board and put the hurt at the back of my mind.

29. A NEW CHALLENGE

In 2005 I retired from teaching. At last freedom reigned. No more being ruled by the bell announcing the beginning and ending of classes. I was free to create my new beginnings. Time on my own was never a problem. I was always a woman who liked to travel alone, while having a loving circle of friends. I didn't always need company to navigate the world, but I did like company.

However, my first day of freedom from the ties of a school timetable unsettled me hugely. I felt like a ship let loose from its shelter, with no harbour for protection. That first September morning in 2005 when I knew all my friends and colleagues were back at work, I walked up the Rathmines Road to visit the supermarket. A sea of women with worried faces passed me by, all of them carrying shopping bags, all of them scurrying by like wound-up people on the treadmill of domesticity.

No, I couldn't join this group of people; it was like I was having an existential breakdown. When I got home I reached for the telephone directory and phoned UCD to ask for details about their daytime courses. They told me about 'The Short Story and Beyond' being taught by Susan Knight. It was the 'Beyond' of this title that attracted me; it was new territory. I felt like a teenager reaching out for a new identity, a new skin.

The classes were on the Carysfort College campus in Blackrock. Here I met men and women of all ages. Susan, a brilliant facilitator, knew how to stimulate a mixed group and initiate then in the practice of writing. She is also a brilliant writer with a large body of work to her credit. Every week at the end of class she would give us a prompt, a trigger to write a story for the following week. During the writing of these stories I discovered that I was exercising a part of my brain that must have been dormant for a long time. It was another wake-up call. Another part of myself that I had neglected.

Susan would say, 'Writing is all about rewriting and editing.' I thought, yes, that's just like the way I want to continue my life. Do I need to rewrite my life? The answer is yes—and no. I can't recreate the past, but I can come to terms with it. I can come to understand it. I can reframe it, but I cannot edit out the facts. Now, I am learning to live with those facts and to forgive myself for my mistakes.

Since retiring from teaching I have made many new friends, but still treasure those from my younger days. As the weeks of Susan's course went by, our group blossomed in many ways, and new friendships were formed that have endured the passage of time.

For the first time in my life I realised through these classes that I had an insatiable desire to nourish my own creativity in as many ways as was possible. For years I had been in the role of assisting in other people's development, other peoples' children. It was now my time—time to edit and rewrite. But there were some parts of my life I couldn't rewrite.

At one stage I had visited the Family Planning to see if I was still fertile. The woman there laughed at me and said, 'Are you joking, at your age?' I was forty-eight at the time, but the urge to give birth again was stimulated after meeting Elizabeth. The phrase 'damaged goods' came to mind. Yes, I had to admit that for my fertile years I had lived in a society that labelled me thus and now the damage was done. It was too late to give birth to another soul.

Now I'm giving birth to myself; the journey still goes on despite the ageing process.

The year I met Elizabeth, 1993, was the year I moved into my new apartment overlooking the cricket field and tennis courts in Rathmines. A group of women played tennis there every Thursday morning and I became a member of the club. Not only was I learning the rudiments of tennis, but I was becoming part of a tribe of women who enjoyed life to the full, who celebrated each other's achievements.

I had no contact with Elizabeth but I would hear snippets about her through the grapevine of friends of friends. One happy message came to me about her wedding day. It came on a very sad day, the day my brother-in-law Dermot was being buried in Galway. I thought about Elizabeth in her white dress walking up the aisle as poor Dermot was being lowered into his grave, my sister Eileen and her children shedding tears at his graveside. It was a reminder of the cycle of life, the cycle of endings and beginnings, the turning of the seasons and facing every new day that was gifted to us.

Retirement was a word I could never embrace, and I recoiled when people used it to describe my social status. It is true that a single person is identified by their profession, and I did feel somewhat at a loss, but I wasn't prepared to settle for oblivion.

My writing practice continued with Susan's classes and with attending other writing workshops in the Irish Writers Centre and at various literary festivals like the Listowel Writers' Week. One morning I heard a radio interview with a woman who had completed the MPhil in Creative Writing at Trinity College, and I was captivated by her account of her time there. She described herself as a fledgling writer, and I knew exactly what she meant, because that was what I was, a person who was learning how to fly again. An emerging writer, not young but still growing. My God, but doesn't it take a lifetime to grow up?

Within weeks of my application to Trinity, I was excited to learn that I had secured a place on their 2007-2008 course. It was during this year that I learned how to write to a deadline—or should I say it was the deadline that forced me to produce written work.

As well as new beginnings, there were, unfortunately, endings. This was the year that Brian died. Elizabeth had only met him once as an adult, and after that meeting she decided that she only needed one father in her life and that was the one who cherished her from childhood.

My dilemma was whether I should tell Elizabeth. She had a right to know, but she had told me that she didn't want any more contact with me. A friend who knew her family informed Elizabeth's mother. Celia and Carmel came with me to his memorial service in Donnybrook church. From the back of the church I could recognise his wife. The young woman with her had to be her daughter because she bore a strong resemblance to Elizabeth.

EPILOGUE

In 2021, after almost a twenty-year silence, the first email contact emerged from Elizabeth. She wrote: 'How are you? You must be upset with all the revelations about the Mother and Baby Homes?'

She was the first person to ask me how I felt about the published report by the Commission of Investigation in January, 2021, highlighting yet another injustice to the 500 women whose testimonies were ignored. This report shocked an apparently docile Irish society, revealing the scandal of illegal adoption stories and the ill-treatment of the women in mother-and-baby institutions.

After this initial contact, an exchange of emails began. The dam of silence was burst and her hurts came tumbling out. She cited many reasons for the estrangement, ones that were not either remembered by me or ones that were misunderstood. We were, after all, two people coming together out of separate histories. One of the reasons she thought that our relationship ended was that we dived into each other too forcefully during those first ten years. It was true we fell in love with each other, and I have to admit that I experienced a certain type of madness. But more true to say a certain type of an out-of-body existence. It was a bit like being presented with a reality where I had to discover which role to play. It was like being auditioned by a young woman who found me unsuitable for the character she had in her mind.

It must have been a difficult time for her also. There is a constellation of people and families who are affected in any one adoption story and it casts a long shadow.

'Why didn't she tell us?' and 'Why didn't they notice?' It's all in the past now, but the questions still remain. The hurt still remains. It is really a story without an end.

We had been let down on so many levels. She had said many times, 'You were robbed.' This was also the year that she had access to her birth certificate for the first time in her life, only to discover that the mother's name was not mine but a mishmash of names Brian had made up. It has to be said that Elizabeth was also robbed. In a film by Bernie Masterson about gay women, one woman was asked what was the most difficult part of her life, coming out as a gay person or being adopted. Her reply was being adopted, because it is an act that is done to you—being separated from your roots at the beginning of your life without your permission.

To say the umbilical cord is never broken is true, it is always embedded deeply in the soul, but when the birth disconnection is broken, repairing it is like trying to reassemble a perfectly made cobweb.

I also applied to have access to my records. The handwritten letter written by a nun from St. Patrick's to a Sister Josephine in the mother house of the Sisters of Charity in Paris was very moving.

> *...At present I have a very, very nice unmarried mother who told her parents that she was going to Paris for some months to see 'the world.' Unfortunately, she does not know anyone there who would look after her mail for her. She says her mother is not familiar with the Miraculous Medal or Green Scapular and would not recognise your address. I do hope that this will not lead to a good deal of difficulty if this girl, Mary Herbert's mother writes to 140, Rue du Bac. Could you possibly intercept the letter, Sister please, and re-address it to here?*

Among the many other documents sent to me by Tusla, some of which were redacted, was a Certificate of Baptism stating that Brónagh Seána Herbert was born on the July 18 and was baptised according to the rite of the Catholic Church by Rev. Patrick Finn, the local parish priest from Our Lady of Christians, Navan Road, Dublin, on the July 22, 1967. This was something I was not informed of even though I was still a resident in the home. The sponsor was a woman unknown to me.

There were many lies told to many parties in relation to our story. The true facts about the final lie was told to me by Elizabeth. In 2022 she said, 'In the interests of historical accuracy, there's something I have to tell you.'

The photo of her as a baby that the nuns had sent to me after my phone call asking to have my baby back in 1967, and one that had pride of place on my mantlepiece, was not my baby. Elizabeth had discovered that the nuns had a stock of baby photos for people like me who regretted turning their backs on their babies. Elizabeth's mother did in fact send a photo to St. Patrick's, but the photo I was sent and cherished was of someone else's baby. That photo still remains on my mantlepiece beside the photo of Elizabeth at the age of twenty-six, the one she sent me before our first meeting in 1993.

There are so many families affected by adoption. The primary one has to be the adoptive family. In the case of Elizabeth, she entered a family where she became a third child to her new parents and a new sister to her two older siblings. Early in our relationship I had the pleasure of meeting both her parents and later her brother and sister. They were very warm towards me. Elizabeth's family is her story and not mine.

My family was also affected, but not until I revealed the fact to them twenty-six years later. It was my secret up until then. Enforced secrecy isolates you, and it takes years to understand what that does to a life and to all the people around you. Secrets imprison the human spirit and arrest emotional growth, and that is why I had such empathy with the people I taught inside the prison walls. Their lives were on hold while serving the imposed sentence. I too feel I have done my time, and now I feel a sense of release.

The passage of time though has been good to me, and I am very grateful for the life I have now. My tribe include my siblings and my friends—friends who are interested in me alone and ask me what I'm writing ; friends who accompany me on my journey of creativity and who acknowledge me for the person I've become; friends who know my story and listen when I need to talk; friends who know that I love my daughter despite our estrangement.

Despite the airing of Elizabeth's accusations against me, it would appear there is no closing of the account with her, and that is a heavy burden of regret for me.

During our happy days together, that first decade we met, Elizabeth sent me a card from Paris, two people sitting outside a cafe having tea together, one an elderly woman and a younger woman and she said on the card, 'This will be you and me in a few years time.' It is a sadness I carry with me and it will never go away. But I forgive myself, and Elizabeth said that she forgave me also. Life goes on, it must go on.

My present life now often takes me on walks down the banks of the Grand Canal near my home. The weeping willow touches the water as if to say, 'I see my reflection in the water and I'm enjoying the act of spreading my limbs. This is where I'm rooted but my branches can see in all directions.' On the other side of the canal in those long front gardens are cherry trees blazing their blossoms and reminding me that although physical beauty has its time, there is another life to be had, the one we hold inside of us. I walk on with my friend until we come to the bronze figure of Patrick Kavanagh on the seat just before Baggot Street Bridge. He is in pristine condition. Nobody dares to defile his figure, such is the respect he attracts. The opening words of his poem Canal Bank Walk soothe me every time.

Leafy-with-love banks and the green waters of the canal
Pouring redemption for me that I do the will of God...

I continue my walk ,crossing more bridges until I arrive at the basin where the canal water flows into the river Liffey, waiting to be drawn into the wide-open Irish sea.

ACKNOWLEDGEMENTS.

The idea for this book was born when I attended a class on memoir writing given by Ivy Bannister at the Irish Writers' Centre. The big question was, 'Who and what shapes our lives?' And so, my journey down the years began in 2020, but I would not have travelled far without the generous encouragement of that wonderful teacher and writer. Thank you, Ivy. You kept me on track, and without you this book would never have happened.

Feedback and encouragement are the oxygen that sustain the writing act, and I was fortunate to have had people on my side who gave me of their time. People such as:

- Herbie Brennan and Jacquie Burgess who bolstered my confidence when it was lacking.
- Susan Knight, my first and most influential teacher who generously read versions of the book and offered me her invaluable insights.
- Lucille Redmond, who edited the first draft and contributed rich information.
- Muriel Bolger, a woman I had the pleasure of meeting in the Tyrone Guthrie Centre, who read the final draft and whose insights added to the work.

So many of my friends either read sections or listened to me discuss elements of the book, and I hope I haven't omitted any of them here: Colette McAndrew, Ruth Kenny, Carmel Lynch, Sheila Murray, Eva Kenny, Monique Walsh, Eileen Graham, Ann Murphy, Celia de Fréine, Janet Pierce, David Storan Byrne, Gabriel Byrne, Anne Weber, Bernie Masterson, Helena Powell, Fíona Bushe, Paddy Bushe, Cathy Sweeney, Loretto Wrynn, Michael King, Statia Somers, Emer Sweeney, Alan Hayes, Sibylle McGovern and the WEB Writers' Group.

Thank you to my family for their patience in bearing with me not knowing what I would reveal to the world.

Lastly, thanks to Maurice Sweeney, my extraordinary publisher at Menma Books, for his insights and his kindness.